Co

Publisher's Note

Preface

∽ Opening Comments ∼

1

Talking Directly to the Person Who is Responsible for Spreading The View of Japan as the "Bad Guy"

THE WITHDRAWN

SECRET

BEHIND

THE

RAPE

OF

NANKING

A SPIRITUAL CONFESSION
BY **IRIS CHANG**

Videotaped June 12, 2014
Happy Science General Headquarters, Tokyo

RYUHO OKAWA
IRH Press

IRH PRESS USA INC.
New York
Distributed by Midpoint Trade Books. www.midpointtrade.com

Library of Congress Cataloging-in-Publication Data
ISBN 13: 978-1-942125-00-6
ISBN 10: 1942125003

Printed in the United States of America

5

I Was Used by
The United States to Bash Japan

6

The Truth Behind the
Made-up Estimate of 300,000 people

7

"I Was Drugged and Led To Commit Suicide"

8

The Hidden Background to The book, *The Rape of Nanking*

9

The Reality Seen By Iris Chang After Her Death

10

"I Want My Book
To be Taken Out of Print"

11

"There Was No Nanking Massacre"
"I'm Sorry"

❧ Closing Comments ❧

12

After Receiving the Spiritual Message
From Iris Chang

Afterword

Publisher's Note

Sometimes a single book can determine how the international society sees history, as well as give a great impact on international relations. If a fabricated history had spread throughout the world and is subjecting the citizens of a particular country to humiliation that they don't deserve, then speaking from international justice and humanitarian viewpoints, such history must be rewritten in an objective and impartial manner. There is a phrase, "History is written by the victors." The usual process is that, after a war, the victors come up with a one-sided historical view that is advantageous to them and historical researchers of later generations gradually make corrections to it.

Nevertheless, sometimes history takes a sudden turn due to revelations from Heaven. This book is a rare example of that. The author of a book which gave a great impact on the historical view that had spread throughout the international society today confessed the truth regarding the content of her book and its background, just 10 years after her death, in a form of a spiritual message.

The Nanking Massacre and *The Rape of Nanking*

One of the biggest cases, with the possibility of fabrication,

11

that happened in the 20th century was the so-called "Nanking Massacre." It is said that, after the Japanese army took over Nanking, China on December 13, 1937, Japanese soldiers apparently massacred over 200,000 civilians and prisoners of war, and raped 20,000 women, in a span of several weeks after taking over the city. The first case in which this was brought up was at the International Military Tribunal for the Far East [Tokyo Trials] that began in 1946. The victor nations condemned the massacre as an inhumane act by the Japanese army during World War II.

China has been rapidly gaining strength in recent years and is about to establish its status as a hegemony. At the same time, the Chinese government is taking the Nanking Massacre up to a whole new level in the international society. In June 2014, the Chinese government filed an application with UNESCO to register the history materials regarding the Nanking Massacre and the comfort women as "Memories of the World."

The Rape of Nanking, which came out in 1997 – roughly half a century after the Tokyo Trials – is a book that greatly contributed to creating this trend. Due to, the term "Nanking Massacre" has recently resurfaced and spread rapidly throughout the world, starting with the United States. The author of that book, Iris Chang, was an aspiring 29-year-old Chinese-American journalist at the time it was published. *The Rape of Nanking* was her second book. Sources say that, since the content of the book was so sensational in that the inhumane acts of the Japanese were like the Holocaust carried out by the German Nazis, as well as her status as a young and beautiful female author, the book was on *The New York Times* Bestseller list for 10 weeks and that 500,000 copies of the book were sold. [In *The Rape of Nanking*, she wrote that approximately 300,000 people of Nanking were massacred and 20,000 to 80,000 women were raped. These numbers are even greater than those reported at the Tokyo Trials.]

Questions regarding the Nanking Massacre

Currently, however, the credibility of the Nanking Massacre is under strong suspicion by researchers in Japan and in the world. Many testimonies at the Tokyo Trials were used as groundless evidence, starting with the massacre of 200,000 people. What is more, the majority of those were information by ear.

In reality, the Japanese army occupied Nanking in accordance with international rules. It was done in an extremely orderly fashion; it was far from "a mass slaughter of civilians." At the ongoing FIFA World Cup in Brazil, Japanese fans picked up litter in the stands. Their excellent manners surprised, and was praised from, the world. In the aftermath of the 2011 Tohoku earthquake and tsunami, Japanese people in the Tohoku region persevered and helped each other through difficulties, and the disaster-stricken areas did not turn into lawless land. The world was impressed by this. These are examples of long-time national character and moral traditions of the Japanese people – people of a country that is the home of the world's oldest imperial household, and also the people who have strongly believed in Buddhism and Shintoism. Could these Japanese people really have done such inhumane and cruel acts, as portrayed at the Tokyo Trials and in *The Rape of Nanking*?

The Rape of Nanking has been brought up and argued by many experts as a ludicrous book, from the time it was published. The photos used in the book as records of cruel acts by the Japanese army are all photos that have been taken from elsewhere, completely irrelevant to the Japanese soldiers and Nanking. Experts have also pointed out that modifications have been made to some of these photos, too. (In 2005, a book titled *Nanking Jiken Shoko Shashin Wo Kensho Suru* [Identifying the "Photographic Evidence" of the Nanking Incident], Tokyo: Soshisha Publishing, 2005, by Professor Shudo Higashinakano, was published. This book proved that there was not a single photo that could be used as valid evidence of the Nanking Massacre.) In the end, it was made clear that they were all fake photos used for propaganda.

In addition, according to the historical sources available at the time, the population of Nanking was roughly 200,000 people. Some people say that the population increased to roughly 250,000 people, thanks to the restoration of order by the Japanese army, one month after the fall of Nanking. Furthermore, even though Chiang Kai-shek, the supreme leader at that time, made a claim to the League of Nations that the Japanese army wrongfully bombarded and destroyed homes of civilians during the attack on Nanking, he had not filed a single claim regarding the Nanking Massacre. See Shoichi Watanabe, *Nihon To Shina - 1500 Nen No Shinjitsu* [Japan and China, Truth of 1500 Years] (Kyoto: PHP Institute, 2006).

The Rape of Nanking was published and, while Chang received positive remarks, she also received criticisms. In 2003, she published her third book but it was not successful; Chang apparently fell into depression at this time. She was found dead in her car in November 2004. Chang was writing her fourth book during this period. It is said that she shot herself in the head with a gun.

Iris Chang's spiritual confession

Despite all the debate going on about this, university

professors and historians in the U.S. and China today still use *The Rape of Nanking* as a resource for writing their papers. There are plenty of people who believe in the content of the book without any doubt, just as it is written. It is quite difficult to determine the authenticity of the Nanking Massacre, which is a story of something that is said to have happened almost 80 years ago, because there are two sides to this: what the Japanese are saying, and the ulterior motives of China, America and the victor nations. This is also an issue related to the legitimacy of World War II as well as that of the post war regime.

In order to provide a powerful material in identifying this issue, we have published "The Secret Behind *The Rape of Nanking*," a book revealing Chang's current state and the strong possibility of a conspiracy behind *The Rape of Nanking*. This was done by a method unheard of: summoning the spirit of Iris Chang from the spirit world, 10 years after her death.

Regardless of whether or not you believe in a spiritual message phenomenon, as an individual human being, you cannot remain unmoved by her tears of apology and the truth in her plea, both coming from the bottom of her heart. And you will probably ask yourself, "How can I answer her desperate plea?"

What is a spiritual message?

A spiritual message is the act of relaying the message of a spirit by someone who possesses spiritual abilities. In history, Jesus Christ received the words of the Heavenly Father and told them to the people; Moses received the Ten Commandments from God; and Muhammad received revelation from Allah and wrote them down as the Koran – these are a few forms of spiritual message. The Buddhist scriptures say that Shakyamuni Buddha had spiritual conversations with gods and devils, too. There have been many others in history who possessed spiritual abilities and conveyed the words of spirits.

Happy Science's spiritual messages are not only from the spirits of people who lived in the past, but are also from the guardian spirits of living people [A guardian spirit resides in the spirit world, and is a part of the consciousness of the living person, as well as a past life of that person. See *The Laws of the Sun*, New York: IRH Press, 2013, and http://global.the-liberty.com for more]. In these messages, you can see the characteristic as a religion that is quite different from world religions and spirit mediums: the names and characters of those spirits are identified, and the spiritual messages are given in an extremely clear manner. Neither Jesus nor Muhammad was able to discern the characters of different spirits this clearly. If you compare Master Ryuho

Okawa's spiritual abilities to those of the above, you can assume that he has the highest spiritual abilities in the history of humankind.

Master Ryuho Okawa can summon such spirits at his will and make them give spiritual messages through his own body or the body of another channeler. Some spirits are able to use Master Okawa's language center and give spiritual messages in Japanese. Master's own consciousness is retained throughout the spiritual message, which is something that differs from common spirit mediums. The majority of his spiritual messages are publicly recorded in front of a live audience. Videos of these spiritual messages are made public, and the spiritual messages are published as books, too.

The spiritual messages of more than 200 spirits have been recorded by Master Okawa since 2010, and the majority of these have been published. Spiritual messages from the guardian spirits of living politicians such as U.S. President Obama, Japanese Prime Minister Shinzo Abe and Chinese General Secretary Xi Jinping, as well as spiritual messages sent from the spirit world by Jesus Christ, Thomas Edison, Mother Teresa, Steve Jobs and Nelson Mandela are just a tiny pack of spiritual messages that were published so far. Domestically, in Japan, these spiritual messages are being read by a wide range of politicians and mass media, and the high-level contents of these books are delivering an impact even more on politics, news and public opinion. In recent years, there have been spiritual messages recorded in English, and English translations are being done on the spiritual messages given in Japanese. These have been published overseas, one after another, and have started to shake the world.

As of June 2014, the total number of books by Master Okawa, including the Spiritual Messages series, surpassed 1,600. This quantity, as well as the contents of these books, is proof that he possesses the highest spiritual abilities of humankind.

Why spiritual messages are a must for the human race

There are two main reasons why Master Okawa is conducting and publishing countless spiritual messages at an amazing pace. One is to prove the existence of the spirit world. Sages of mankind such as Shakyamuni Buddha, Socrates, Jesus Christ, Muhammad and Newton all recognized the existence of spirits and the spirit world in which God and Buddha reside. Due to the development in technology, there are many people who do not believe in the existence of the spirit world in the modern society. However, a global movement to believe in the spirit world is occurring now through near-death experiences, spiritualism, etc. What lies at the very center of this movement and is making the most thorough attempt at proving the existence of the spirit world, is the spiritual messages series conducted by Master Okawa.

The other reason is to provide the supplies mankind needs in order to think about the future of Earth. The path that humans should take can be searched for by learning the ideas of, and at times learning valuable lessons from the mistakes made by, the spirits of past religious leaders, politicians and scientists. In addition, by disclosing the true thoughts and feelings of leading figures who are alive, we can foresee the direction that international politics and economy are proceeding in, and detect and warn of the crises.

We hope that you, too, will read the spiritual messages series by Happy Science and awaken to the eternal Truth that your essence is an imperishable soul. We want you to find out the truth in history that has been hidden from you, what is at the depths of the current world affairs and, also, we want you to make a commitment from your conscience to shift the reality of global society toward a future that the human race should live in.

Learning the secrets of the Nanking Massacre and Iris Chang, by reading this book, you are taking the first step toward that goal.

Preface

I feel that the publication of this book is extremely significant in the sense that it rewrites the political system of post war Japan and redraws our future global strategy map as well.

Fabricating the so-called "Nanking Massacre" as a crime against humanity on the level of the Nazi Holocaust and chaining Japan in the shackles of Article 9[*] of the Japanese Constitution are the national strategies of China today, as well as its strategies for Asia and Oceania. As long as the United States of America believes in this "Great Nanking Incident," China can deceive the United States into sharing the same fate.

In today's climate, with Vietnam, the Philippines and Australia all requesting defense cooperation from Japan and with Chinese air force jets threatening and closing in on Japanese Self-Defense Force jets as close as 30 meters, Japan's philosophy simply must change. If it turns out that Iris Chang's *The Rape of Nanking*, which became the origin for the view of Japan as the "bad guy," was actually false, it would mark a major turning point in history.

> *Ryuho Okawa*
> *Master & CEO of Happy Science Group*
> *June 12, 2014*

---

[*]The article that states the non-maintenance of the armed forces and the renunciation of war.

Iris Chang (1968 - 2004)

A Chinese–American journalist. She was born in New Jersey, U.S.A. and grew up in Illinois. She majored in journalism at the University of Illinois. After working at the Associated Press and the Chicago Tribune, Chang pursued her graduate studies at Johns Hopkins University. In addition to publishing the *The Rape of Nanking* in 1997, she compared the Nanking incident to the Holocaust and traveled to many cities, giving lectures calling for "a thorough pursuit and inquiry into Japan's war crimes." Chang was found dead in her car in 2004. The cause of death was concluded to be suicide by gun.

Interviewers:[*]

Soken Kobayashi
Vice Chairperson of Public Relations and Risk Management

Jiro Ayaori
Advanced Executive Director of Happy Science
Chief Editor, *The Liberty*

Yukihisa Oikawa
Director General of Foreign Affairs
Happiness Realization Party

*The opinions of the spirits do not necessarily
reflect those of Happy Science Group.*

---

[*] Interviewers' professional titles represent their positions at the time of the interview. Their names are listed in the order that they appear in the transcript.

1

Talking Directly to the Person Who is Responsible for Spreading The View of Japan as the "Bad Guy"

Putting the Nanking Massacre dispute to rest, Once and for all

RYUHO OKAWA:

We recently recorded the spiritual messages from the guardian spirit of international politics scholar Kiichi Fujiwara.* On that occasion, he said, "If you want to talk about the Nanking Massacre, you should receive a spiritual message from Iris Chang. If she really researched everything herself and told the truth, then she should be an angel now. If she said things that weren't true, then she will be in Hell. Looking at that should tell you what happened, so you can check it for yourself." He said like this as if it was no business of his. But I thought that, actually, doing what he said was definitely one way to find out.

But for some reason, when I tried to read material on

---

* See Ryuho Okawa, *Kiki No Jidai No Kokusai Seiji* [International Politics in an Age of Crisis] (Tokyo: IRH Press, 2014).

the Nanking incident, my head would start to hurt and my body would feel heavy, and I would just feel bad all over. So I wasn't too motivated to get into this issue. So I left it alone for a while.

Yesterday I thought once again, "maybe tomorrow..." and read up to 90 pages of *The Rape of Nanking* at night. But once again, my head started to hurt. I just couldn't finish the entire 260 some odd pages, and went to sleep thinking, "Well, maybe another day" [*laughs*].

Then, around 3:00 in the morning, Professor Shoichi Watanabe [see Figure 1] appeared in my dreams and stayed with me until dawn. I think the visitation was not only by his own spirit, but his guardian spirit also came, and we talked about lots of different things.

One part of me thought that perhaps he was worried about the establishment of Happy Science University.

Figure 1.
Shoichi Watanabe (1930 – present): Japanese scholar of the English language, and critic. Professor emeritus at Sophia University. Aside from his expertise in English language, he is also giving out many conservative opinions via books and magazines.

But another part of me wondered if, just maybe, he came to give me the push after I put down *The Rape of Nanking* and went to sleep without making a firm decision as to whether or not I would conduct a spiritual research into it today.

After all, the Nanking incident is a major issue and a theme that Professor Watanabe is pursuing as his life work. Although it may be possible to refute in many ways about this event, people who refute may be feeling frustrated since they cannot present any "hard evidence." So they seem to be unable to put it to rest.

Actually, I researched into the comfort women issue* through spiritual messages, and I also investigated fairly thoroughly into the characters of South Korean President Park Geun-hye and Chinese President Xi Jinping through the spiritual messages from their guardian spirits. Through these attempts, I made judgments about them, and things have generally turned out as I predicted [see Figure 2].

Regarding Mr. Xi Jinping, we Happy Science put forth statements about his character and what he is likely to do

---

* South Korea alleges that the Japanese Army forcibly collected 200,000 Korean women to serve as "sex slaves" during World War II. There were definitely military brothels in army posts, but there is no concrete proof that the Japanese Army was involved in that.

since even before he became China's president. And what we have said has generally come to pass regarding that.

Currently, countries like Vietnam, the Philippines, and Australia are showing interest in forming relations with Japan to defend themselves against China. Looking at this, I cannot agree with the opinion that China has suddenly strengthened its resolve and become militaristic in response to a hard-line Abe administration. Instead, what we are looking at here is the emergence of the real deal after a preparation period of over a decade, perhaps even close to 20 years now.

Figure 2.
See Ryuho Okawa, *The Truth of Nanking and Comfort Women Issues: A Spiritual Reading into World War II by Edgar Cayce* (New York: IRH Press, 2014), *Why I am Anti-Japan: Interviewing the Guardian Spirit of Korean President Park Geun-hye* (New York: IRH Press, 2014), *Kami Ni Chikatte Jugun Ianfu Wa Jitsuzai Shitaka* [Can You Swear to God that "Comfort Women" Really Existed?] (Tokyo: IRH Press, 2013), *Sekai Kotei Wo Mezasu Otoko* [The Man Who Aims to Rule the World] (Tokyo: IRH Press, 2010), and *China's Hidden Agenda: The Mastermind Behind the Anti-American and Anti-Japanese Protests* (New York: IRH Press, 2012).

Used as a "reverse-brainwashing strategy" of China, Who conceals facts about the Tiananmen incident?

OKAWA:

Iris Chang was a young woman of Chinese descent. Her parents immigrated to the United States, where Chang was born. However, she was born in 1968, which makes her 12 years younger than me. More to the point, she was born 23 years after the war ended, making her part of a generation that knows absolutely nothing of the war.

In *The Rape of Nanking*, she writes that her parents made it a point to talk to her frequently about the Nanking incident since childhood. However, I think that she also wrote that neither of her parents actually saw the incident. In other words, they did not see or experience the event, but had heard about it in the form of a story.

Chang studied journalism at university, worked as a fledgling journalist for some time, and wrote *The Rape of Nanking* at 29 years of age. I believe it was her second book. And the funding apparently came from people of Chinese descent.

Chang said something along the lines that, though the Holocaust by Germany is well-known in the United

States, almost no one there, or across the world, knows about the Nanking incident. She claimed that everyone knows that a large number of people died in the Great Tokyo Air Raids and the atomic bombing of Hiroshima and Nagasaki, but no one knows about the Nanking incident, so she has a duty to tell people about it.

Also, it is worth noting that this book came out in 1997.

Chang claimed that the reason this Nanking Massacre incident was not known about was that, after World War II,— the Cold War structure and an antagonistic "Japan and the U.S. vs. China and the USSR" relationship came into being, effectively hiding the incident from the spotlight. Her idea was that when the USSR crumbled and the Cold War ended, the facts about the incident came out into the light. And she wrote, whether she is aware of it or not, that the Tiananmen incident* occurred in China in 1989, and in the process of a variety of information regarding that incident coming out onto the international scene, facts about the Nanking Massacre also surfaced.

---

* A democracy movement in China that happened in June 1989. The civilian protesters including university students, factory workers and citizens occupied the Tiananmen Square and called for the democratization of China. The Chinese government condemned the protests as a "counter-revolutionary riot," and suppressed them and their supporters with some 300,000 troops. It resulted in numerous numbers of deaths.

However, as we have already stated on the Happy Science web-show called *The Fact*, it is strange indeed to say, "The Tiananmen incident occurred and then the Nanking issue was discovered as a result." In fact, that is exactly the style that China uses in their propaganda today. It is believed that some thousand students, or maybe even in the range of some ten to twenty thousand students, were killed in the Tiananmen incident. But the truth is being concealed, and we still do not know the total count even today. Information is being controlled and the Chinese government suppresses all related news from being published or broadcast.

Chang claims that the Nanking issue came out in the research process of communicating with Chinese people living abroad. But the truth is that there is an extremely high chance that this is an example of the Chinese "reverse-brainwashing strategy" wherein they slant every story to make Japan look like "the villain."

Was Chang manipulated to support the view Of Japan as "the villain" in era of growing ties Between the U.S. and China?

OKAWA:
Japanese weekly news magazines used to feature blurbs

like, "Who is this Iris Chang, this 'anti-Japan Joan of Arc'?" I get the very strong feeling that she was a young and inexperienced journalist in her twenties who was given information and made to write, and was used as a resource to strengthen a campaign in the United States to paint Japan as "the villain." I think she was manipulated.

At that time, from 1992 to 2000, the United States was headed by the Clinton administration. During that period, the United States and China built extremely strong ties, and the amount of trade was immense. China was experiencing a progressively rising surge in economic growth. Since the USSR had just crumbled, China was probably afraid of breaking apart itself. And this is most likely why China took the policy of enhancing central control on military and strengthening its militarism, while simultaneously expanding trade with the United States in a bid to become an economic power to prevent itself from succumbing to the same fate as the USSR.

At the same time, Japan's long 20-year protracted slump started. This, of course, traces its origins to the 90s. Around that time the Japanese government issued an official apology through the "Kono Statement" followed by the "Murayama Statement,"* which generated the general atmosphere of admitting wrongdoings on the part of the Japanese government, an atmosphere which I feel was taken advantage of. So, some sort of conspiracy may have been set against Japan around 1997.

In those times, China was still able to play the victim. However, starting around 2010 and onwards, China has started to lose its reputation as a victim and began to take on the impression of being "a wolf." Nevertheless, it would be true to say that they have had a strategic approach, while Japan didn't.

The Nanking Massacre incident came into the worldwide spotlight after this book [*The Rape of Nanking*] was published in 1997. At that time, Happy Science had just opened the Head Temples in Utsunomiya, Tochigi Prefecture. We built Head Temple *Shoshinkan*, followed by Head Temple *Miraikan*.[†] This was the time period in which the book was first published. It went on to become a best seller, selling around five hundred thousand copies. It became famous in the United States, and was soon well-known worldwide as well.

---

[*] Kono Statement: A statement released in August 1993 by then-Chief Secretary of Cabinet Yohei Kono, in relation to the comfort women issue, expressing "sincere apologies and remorse."

Murayama Statement: A statement released in August 1995 by then-Prime Minister Tomiichi Murayama. Its aim was to apologize formally to Asian countries where Japan governed or trespassed by the Japanese Army.

[†] Two of four Head Temples of Happy Science. *Shoshinkan* and *Miraikan* are sacred places where prayers, spiritual training and worship take place.

However, at the tender age of 36, in 2004, the author began to debilitate herself with all sorts of substances, and finally wound up committing suicide with a gun. It was a mysterious death. Some have suggested that she could have been suffering from the weight of her own conscience, while others say that she had reached her limits as a journalist.

Apparently, while researching and writing about the "Bataan Death March" imposed by Japanese forces, she began to sense her limits as a journalist in the sense that, after conducting actual inquiries and writing, she could not mold the information into a format that would support the conclusions she was seeking. And this was causing her emotional pain.

The truth is, however, we do not know if she actually committed suicide, or if she was silenced. The whole thing feels strange to me, so I feel that we cannot entirely rule out the possibility that she could have been silenced.

I want to prevent China from applying to register The Nanking Massacre as a "Memory of the World"

OKAWA:
Now let's look at the current environment surrounding

Japan. Our ruling party is claiming that Japan, Vietnam, the Philippines, Australia and other countries need to cooperate with the U.S. military to lay down a defense system, and is steering toward achieving it. However, the opposition parties and the New Komeito Party are vehemently opposed to this.

On the other hand, because this is a time when Japan's right to collective self-defense[*] is being discussed, China is attempting to register the records of the "Nanking Massacre" and what South Korea is calling the "military comfort women" incidents as "Memory of the World."[†] And Japan's Chief Cabinet Secretary Yoshihide Suga has entered a plea for the registration application to be retracted.

What is more, recent news reports are talking about Chinese jets closing in on Japanese Self-Defense Force jets at distances of 30 meters. If you are attacked when your jet is just 30 meters away from another, it is impossible for you to make a counterattack in self-defense. Whether the approaching jet chooses to use a machine gun attack or an air-to-air missile, once it locks in on you and fires, your jet will certainly be shot down.

---

[*] A right under the international law that when a country is under an armed attack, the third country that isn't directly being attacked can also cooperate to defend it.

[†] One of the UNESCO's programs launched to facilitate preservation of the world's documentary heritage through the latest digital techniques and to exhibit to researchers and the public.

We do not know if that kind of incident was by accident or intended, but the current situation near the Senkaku Islands suggests, in a sense, that a war could easily break out anytime. And there is also a chance of war breaking out in Vietnam and the Philippines. Within all of this, Japan is still engaged in intense disputes about the law.

But what is the root of all of this? I would say that it lies in the "Nanking Massacre" and "comfort women" issues.

Today's spiritual message will be Extremely important in foretelling where Japan's post-war system is heading to

OKAWA:
We have actually already done a recording session on the comfort women issue in the past.* At that time, we saw through the issue with an Edgar Cayce reading.

Also, the guardian spirit of Mr. Kiichi Fujiwara has said that since the person who wrote *The Rape of Nanking* has passed away, we should be able to record a spiritual message about it.† If we come right out and ask the author about it, and conduct an inquiry into her post

---

* See Ryuho Okawa, *The Truth of Nanking and Comfort Women Issues*, as already cited.
† See Ryuho Okawa, *Kiki no Jidai no Kokusai Seiji* [International Politics in an Age of Crisis] as already cited.

death state, we will probably be able to find out the truth. So I want to try that.

Whenever I try to read the actual book, my head begins to hurt and my body begins to feel heavy, so I have not been able to read the material in any great detail. So what I am going to do is to call forth the author herself and then leave the specifics up to you all [the interviewers].

Iris Chang was born in America, so I assume that she would naturally want to speak in English. But I am sure that for her level of English, I can interpret it as she speaks. So I want to speak in Japanese as much as possible to save time.

There might be something like a half a second or one second lag time, and the Japanese might not be totally natural or perfect, but I want to try to do this in Japanese. If I wind up speaking English at times, please forgive me. In that case, I ask one of the interviewers, Mr. Oikawa, or someone else to handle it.

She is a journalist who graduated from the University of Illinois and passed away at 36 years of age. For a person with that level of education, I should be more than able to cover her vocabulary level. So I think we can do the entire session in Japanese.

I have not spoken to the spirit of Chang yet. If she is still writhing, then we won't be able to speak with her. In that case, it simply cannot be helped.

And also, regarding the specifics of these issues, if the session ends without really any serious or meaningful discussion, we can always call forth someone like Commander Iwane Matsui [see Figure 3] and ask what really happened. But if she tells us everything, then that will be good.

Alright, then, are we all ready to start?

I believe this is an extremely important issue in foretelling where Japan's post-war system is heading to. And in a sense, I think that today's spiritual message will become an immensely valuable resource. If the information

Figure 3.
Iwane Matsui (1878 - 1948): A general of the Imperial Japanese Army and the supreme commander at the battle of Nanking. He was sentenced to death for his responsibility for the battle at the Tokyo War Crimes Tribunal.

recorded in the over 250 editions I have published in our public spiritual message book series is true, then I think you can consider this session to be the truth as well.

The Rape of Nanking by the young female Chinese-American named Iris Chang became a bestseller and has thoroughly inflicted Japan with the reputation of being on the level of the Nazis of the Holocaust. So the question is, are the facts in the book actually correct? The author passed away 10 years ago, so we would like to ask her what she has thought of this matter since returning to the other world, and bring the truth to light.

Though I do not know if she will come right out and admit the truth, I do feel that the truth will come to light gradually through discussion.

Summoning the spirit of Iris Chang

OKAWA:

Alright, then, I will now summon the spirit of Ms. Iris Chang, the author of *The Rape of Nanking*, to Happy Science General Headquarters.

Iris Chang, author of *The Rape of Nanking.*

Iris Chang, author of *The Rape of Nanking.*

I ask you to descend to Happy Science General Headquarters and speak to us the truth that you have grasped in the spirit world.

Iris Chang, author of *The Rape of Nanking*.

Iris Chang, author of *The Rape of Nanking*.

I ask you to descend to Happy Science General Headquarters and reveal to us the truth that you have learned in the spirit world.

[*About 25 seconds of silence.*]

2

I Was Murdered!

"I'm in pain!" cries the spirit of Iris Chang As she appears in tears

IRIS CHANG:
Huff! [*Takes a breath.*]

SOKEN KOBAYASHI:
Are you Ms. Iris Chang?

IRIS CHANG:
Huff, huff... [*Catching her breath.*]

KOBAYASHI:
Your breathing is really ragged.

IRIS CHANG:
Huff, huff, huff...

KOBAYASHI:
What happened to you?

IRIS CHANG:
[*Coughs violently.*]

KOBAYASHI:
Are you in pain?

IRIS CHANG:
[*Coughs violently.*] Ack! Huff, huff, huff, huff….

KOBAYASHI:
Are you ill?

IRIS CHANG:
Ugh, ugh [*grunting in pain*]. Huff, huff, huff…. Oh, oh, oh, oh, oh. Aagh, aagh!

KOBAYASHI:
You look and sound frightened. What is the reason for that? Is it remorse?

IRIS CHANG:
Aagh, aagh, aagh, aagh, ugh. Huff, huff, huff... I'm in pain. Huff, huff, huff...

KOBAYASHI:
Hmm?

IRIS CHANG:
I'm in pain.

KOBAYASHI:
In pain? What could cause you so much suffering?

IRIS CHANG:
Aagh... What, well... What could, what could...?

KOBAYASHI:
Yes? What could it be?

IRIS CHANG:
What could it be... What could it be... Oh! [*Weeps.*]

KOBAYASHI:
You can't accept the condition you're in after death...

IRIS CHANG:
[*Wails loudly.*]

JIRO AYAORI:

We've heard that you committed suicide. Are you unable to understand your condition after that act?

IRIS CHANG:

[*Sobs.*] I don't understand… I don't understand… I don't understand… I don't understand… I don't understand…

Was Somebody Hounding Iris Chang?

AYAORI:

You don't understand? Do you remember the circumstances when you killed yourself?

IRIS CHANG:

Aagh! I was murdered!

KOBAYASHI:

Murdered!

AYAORI:

Were you murdered?

IRIS CHANG:

[*Weeping.*] That's right, I… I was murdered.

KOBAYASHI:
They say a bullet from a pistol pierced your skull.

IRIS CHANG:
Ugh... I was murdered.

KOBAYASHI:
So you were murdered. I suspected as much.

IRIS CHANG:
I was murdered, murdered!

KOBAYASHI:
Murdered by whom?

IRIS CHANG:
I don't know!

KOBAYASHI:
You don't know?

IRIS CHANG:
I don't know.

AYAORI:
There was a suicide note or something like that left at the scene. It said that some organization in the United States

was after you, and that you had nowhere to run to.

IRIS CHANG:
Yes, yes. [*Voice trembling.*] I was being hounded... I don't know! I just don't know.

AYAORI:
You don't know?

The flow of things changed around the time George W. Bush took office

IRIS CHANG:
For a while after I wrote my book, I was a hero, but then strange things started happening around me.

KOBAYASHI:
"Strange things?" Please tell us, specifically.

IRIS CHANG:
The previous... Bush?

KOBAYASHI:
Yes, George W. Bush, the President of the United States at the time.

IRIS CHANG:

Umm. From about the time he took office, the flow of things turned really strange.

KOBAYASHI:

So in 2001.

IRIS CHANG:

I had support from China but... When President Bush, and in Japan, Prime Minister... Koizumi?

KOBAYASHI:

Yes. Jun'ichiro Koizumi was the prime minister at the time.

IRIS CHANG:

Yes. It was around then that things started changing.

KOBAYASHI:

I see.

IRIS CHANG:

The United States' attitude changed a bit. The criticisms from Japan became quite harsh.

KOBAYASHI:

That's true.

IRIS CHANG:

It was about that time that things started to go wrong with China's lobbying.

KOBAYASHI:

Ah, the lobbying started to go wrong.

IRIS CHANG:

Correct.

KOBAYASHI:

So there was quite a bit of lobbying before that.

IRIS CHANG:

The flow of things changed. Somehow I knew clearly that I was being targeted.

KOBAYASHI:

I see.

IRIS CHANG:

I was being targeted, but by whom? A Chinese group? The CIA? The FBI? Or maybe the Japanese mafia?

KOBAYASHI:

I don't think it was the last one.

IRIS CHANG:

I don't know exactly how, but things started to get strange all around me.

KOBAYASHI:

Things seemed strange to you?

I was in their way, so I was silenced

AYAORI:

You were backed by a Chinese lobbying outfit called the Global Alliance for Preserving the History of World War II in Asia [the GA]. But your relations with the GA deteriorated, too, right?

IRIS CHANG:

Aaagh... Aagh, aagh... Well, basically, China and the United States were trying to come together against Japan, but suddenly, the United States and Japan cozied up to each other again. That was when I started to get the feeling that I was in their way.

KOBAYASHI:

I see. So that's how you felt.

IRIS CHANG:

Yes. I felt that I was in danger.

KOBAYASHI:
You felt you were in danger.

IRIS CHANG:
Yes.

YUKIHISA OIKAWA:
When you say you were "in their way," do you mean you were in the way of the United States? Or of the GA?

IRIS CHANG:
I don't know. Maybe I was targeted by Japanese ninjas.

OIKAWA:
[*Laughs bitterly.*] I doubt that. Now, the GA was supporting you. You couldn't have been in their way, no matter how close the United States and Japan got to each other. Do you really think the GA could have been targeting you?

IRIS CHANG:
I just don't know. But I have the feeling they might have silenced me because my book, *The Rape of Nanking*, was a success.

OIKAWA:
I see.

3

Who Was the Instigator of *The Rape of Nanking*?

A flood of protests over "The photos of the Nanking Massacre"

AYAORI:
Could it be that you started to have your own doubts about the things you wrote in *The Rape of Nanking*?

IRIS CHANG:
The objections from Japan were harsh.

OIKAWA:
Yes, they were.

IRIS CHANG:
After the book was published, even before it was translated into Japanese, there were plenty of objections. Then after the Japanese translation came out, I was subjected to terrible verbal condemnation. I felt as if ninjas were going to come from Japan to attack me.

AYAORI:

[*Chuckles.*] Oh no, I think the only attacks from Japan were of the verbal kind.

KOBAYASHI:

When you say you felt you were in their way, wasn't it just that, as a natural consequence, you got the impression that some of the things in your book were lies?

IRIS CHANG:

[*Sobbing.*] People immediately started pointing out things in my book that were contrary to reality.

KOBAYASHI:

Yes, that's true. What did you think about the things they pointed out? And what do you think about them now?

IRIS CHANG:

People said that the photos I presented as "photos of the Nanking Massacre by the Japanese army" were from a different photo collection.

KOBAYASHI:

They all were.

IRIS CHANG:

That was the start of the attacks against me, and they were horrendous. The photos of Japanese tanks entering Nanking and destroying the city...

KOBAYASHI:

Yes.

IRIS CHANG:

"In 1937 that tank hadn't been built yet," and so on [see Figure 4]. My critics attacked me for so many things like that, saying they were contrary to the facts.

I was criticized on many accounts for writing things without sufficient substantiation.

KOBAYASHI:

What do you think about those things now?

Figure 4.
Figure 4 to 7 are images that were used in the book, *The Rape of Nanking*. According to a researcher, the army tank in this picture is the Type 97 Light armored car. The production began in 1938 and deployed in Kumamoto in 1940 for the first time in Japan. Moreover, it is said that the flamethrower was not equipped to this type.

IRIS CHANG:

Well, I was born long after the war ended, so I didn't know the reality, but my parents told me that there had been a massacre in Nanking, so I thought it must be true. So I took things that I thought were proof of that story and wrote about them.

Was the purpose to reduce the American sense of guilt regarding World War II?

KOBAYASHI:

I'd like to ask you something candidly. The book at your left hand is the Japanese translation of *The Rape of Nanking*. At first it wasn't possible to publish it in Japan, but later it was finally published here.

IRIS CHANG:

Oh. Yes.

KOBAYASHI:

It says in this book that you heard this story from your parents. But did you really hear from them about it in detail, as it says in the book?

IRIS CHANG:

No. I guess they weren't really in a position to do that.

KOBAYASHI:

No, they weren't.

IRIS CHANG:

I guess that was a rumor or something like that.

KOBAYASHI:

Because they weren't in a position to obtain such a detailed description as you wrote in your book. The truth is, you didn't really have such an exchange, such a dialogue, with your parents, did you?

IRIS CHANG:

I hate to admit it, but the United States may have changed its understanding of history.

The United States wanted to use the Nanking Massacre to lessen its sense of guilt in engaging in the war against Japan, in attacking Japan – the large-scale massacre committed in the Great Tokyo Air Raid and the dropping of the atomic bombs on Hiroshima and Nagasaki. So we had a common interest. But when George W. Bush became the president, the flow of things started to change.

KOBAYASHI:

Conditions started to change.

IRIS CHANG:
Yes.

AYAORI:
So the United States tried to revive the issue of the Nanking affair in the 1990s?

KOBAYASHI:
During the Clinton administration?

IRIS CHANG:
There were a number of wars after the Korean War and Vietnam War, and then in 2001 there was 9/11. With its experience of fighting with Islam, the United States began strengthening relations with its allies.

KOBAYASHI:
To fight Al Qaeda and so on.

IRIS CHANG:
There's no question that, around that time, the notion that exposing Japan's crimes would benefit the United States fell out of favor.

KOBAYASHI:
Yes, it certainly did.

"I was used by some smart people"

KOBAYASHI:

Before we get into that big-picture discussion of the political situation, I'd like to revisit our earlier question. Did you really hear from your parents the detailed story that appears in your book?

IRIS CHANG:

No. My mother and father were both researchers in the sciences. They didn't really know much about Japanese history. I don't think they knew those things.

KOBAYASHI:

So they didn't know about the events in Nanking?

IRIS CHANG:

I doubt they knew about them in detail. They weren't journalists or historians, so it's unlikely they would have had detailed knowledge.

KOBAYASHI:

Objectively speaking, it seems that you took the things you said you had heard vague rumors about, and used your training as a journalist to invent a story and presented that as a fact.

IRIS CHANG:

Well... I may have been used.

KOBAYASHI:

You have the impression that you were used?

IRIS CHANG:

I have the feeling that there were some smart people who used me.

I was given a lot of misleading photographs

AYAORI:

Do you mean they used you by feeding you a steady stream of photos and other materials related to the events in question?

IRIS CHANG:

That's right. They gave me a lot of material. There were lots of people giving me those things.

OIKAWA:

Who gave you them?

IRIS CHANG:

That was, what? China's...

OIKAWA:
The GA?

IRIS CHANG:
The GA and people like them. They collected material from a wide range of sources. Photos, I mean. There were lots of horrifying photos. Many severed heads, all lined up [see Figure 5].

KOBAYASHI:
Yes.

IRIS CHANG:
Killing people. Many dead people in the river.

KOBAYASHI:
Dead people.

Figure 5.
This photo is said to be, "The severed heads of Nanking victims." But in fact, the public display of the decapitated heads was prohibitted by the Japanese law in 1879 and was not seen thereafter. On the contrary, this kind of customs were still going on in China even in the 1930s. The heads in this picture are most likely victims of China's civil war, political criminals, or mounted bandits killed by the Chinese.

IRIS CHANG:
There were lots of them, those photos. So many...

OIKAWA:
But they all turned out to be made up, right?

IRIS CHANG:
Yes. That hit me quite hard. For example, there was a head chopped off but with a cigarette in its mouth [see Figure 6]. It turned out later that some American had set that up as a joke. Cutting off a head and sticking cigarette in its mouth isn't something that the Japanese people do.

OIKAWA:
No, it isn't.

IRIS CHANG:
So, things like that, and a river filled with corpses [see Figure 7]. The implication was that the Japanese had

Figure 6.
This photo originally appeared in the *Life* magazine on January 10, 1938. The caption stated that the head was of an anti-Japanese Chinese man, and had been placed there on "December 14, just before the fall of Nanking." However, December 14 was after the fall of Nanking. The caption printed in the *Life* magazine strongly suggests that the Japanese military were responsible for this abomination, but there is no concrete evidence. In fact, what are presented as evidence are all questionable.

massacred people in the river, but in reality people who had died in the war were washed up on the shore.

KOBAYASHI:

That was made up, too. An image from a different scene, carried in a Japanese magazine, was cropped and put to a different use.

IRIS CHANG:

That's right, that's right! They were saying things like that, and the tanks shown in the photos hadn't been developed yet.

KOBAYASHI:

Right. Those tanks first appeared on the battlefield three years later. They didn't exist in 1937.

Figure 7.
This photo is used in *The Rape of Nanking* with the caption "Corpses of Nanking citizens were dragged to the banks of the Yangtze and thrown into the river." However, many Chinese soldiers were not dressed in official military uniform; they were dressed as civilians and fought in guerrilla warfare. Therefore, it is highly likely that the corpses washed up ashore in this photo are of Chinese soldiers who died during or drowned in their escape from battle which could have occurred upstream. Contrary to Iris Chang's explanation, Japanese soldiers did not throw the corpses of citizens into the river.

"They palmed off false material on me
And made me write what I wrote"

IRIS CHANG:

Yes, yes, that's right. A lot of facts like that emerged. They palmed off false material on me and made me write what I wrote. I realized that some things were not as they seemed to me.

KOBAYASHI:

So you recognize that they palmed off on you?

IRIS CHANG:

Yes. I was made to write those things.

KOBAYASHI:

Made to write them. OK.

IRIS CHANG:

Journalism should… I was seeking justice. "This is your chance to stand out, to become famous. We'll give you the money and funding. Write the book," they told me. "We'll advertise it to make sure you get publicity," they said. They told me all these good things.

But later, when I was criticized about various things, a lot of different pictures started to emerge.

4

The Story That 350,000 People Were Killed in Nanking Was a Lie

"350,000 victims was a figure far too extreme"

KOBAYASHI:
Just to confirm, you accept that the photos that were put into your hands were fakes?

IRIS CHANG:
I understood they had their feelings and reasons, but I felt that what they made me write was at variance with the facts.

AYAORI:
You've just said that the photos were clearly different from what really happened. What about the other evidence?

IRIS CHANG:
Those were definitely wrong. Before the Japanese army entered Nanking, it engaged the enemy in Shanghai. The Japanese suffered heavy losses, with over 15,000 Japanese soldiers killed. After that the Japanese army entered Nanking. I wrote, "In six weeks in Nanking,

it seems that the Japanese army killed about 350,000 people—between 260,000 and 370,000 people."

I wrote that, because this atrocity took place over just six weeks, it was comparable in scale to the Holocaust or other various atrocities.

KOBAYASHI:

But as the critics pointed out, a German newspaper back then—this was at a time when Germany was a neutral third party with respect to Japan's actions in China—reported that there might be less than 150,000 people in Nanking. How could the Japanese army have killed 300,000 or 350,000 people in Nanking when the city's population was less than 150,000 to begin with? So your lie was exposed right away.

IRIS CHANG:

I wrote that refugees and others had swollen the population of the city to about 550,000, and of these 350,000 were killed. I guess that figure was unreasonable.

KOBAYASHI:

Since this session will be published and used as a resource material, allow me to state the counterargument on this point. You said that refugees entered Nanking from the surrounding area, but in fact, on December

13, 1937, this photo [see Figure 8] of the Japanese army's entry into Nanking shows that, because the battle was drawing near, not a single soul was left in the downtown, the main streets and other districts in Nanking. The photo shows that the city was empty when the Japanese army captured it .

IRIS CHANG:
Yes, so they'd run away…

KOBAYASHI:
So there was no way that so many people could have been killed.

Figure 8.
The Japanese Army entering Nanking on December 13, 1937: "The Ono Unit advances along Zhongshan Road" [original caption in Japanese. The photo was first used in *Shina Jihen Gaho vol. 13* (Pictorial News of the Second Sino-Japanese War vol. 13), published on January 27, 1938].

IRIS CHANG:

It's possible to presume that those who fled were killed. Taking the argument to extremes, I wrote at one point, "300,000 people were killed, leaving only five people." Only the home of a foreign missionary remained, I said. I suppose that was rather extreme.

KOBAYASHI:

It was extreme, embroidered and…

IRIS CHANG:

When that foreign missionary was asked about it, he told, "There had been a lot of people here, but then they are all gone." That would mean "the number of people decreased from 300,000 to five." That's how I ended up writing such a thing.

KOBAYASHI:

"Ended up"? So you admit you shouldn't have written it?

IRIS CHANG:

Well, but I think I have to say that I was made to write it. I was manipulated into writing it that way.

"In Nanking, the Chinese came up with many ruses
To portray the Japanese army as brutes"

KOBAYASHI:

That's right. Among the records, there were reports and documents stating that it was actually Chinese, not Japanese, soldiers who were robbing, looting and assaulting. But you didn't use that evidence.

IRIS CHANG:

I wrote something in line with "The Japanese soldiers deliberately made it look as if the Chinese had done them." But in fact the Chinese did various things like that, too.

KOBAYASHI:

As an author, you admit that?

IRIS CHANG:

They were trying to portray the Japanese as brutes who did all kinds of terrible things.

KOBAYASHI:

Well, as the title of your book is *The Rape of Nanking*, I'll venture to say this: cases of rape certainly occurred, but there are many passages in the source documents that could be read as saying that special agent provocateurs of the Chinese Nationalist Party were actually the ones who committed those acts.

IRIS CHANG:
If the numbers had been small, yes. But the numbers were too large.

So I wrote that, of the 200,000 or 250,000 people who fled to the safe zone, 80,000 or so were women who had been raped. But that would mean virtually all of the women, from the elderly to children. Maybe I shouldn't have bought such a tall tale.

KOBAYASHI:
You admit that?

IRIS CHANG:
Hmm.

KOBAYASHI:
Japan honored a gentlemen's agreement that the Japanese army would not enter the safe zone, you know?

IRIS CHANG:
Hmm. I guess that was out of the question.

KOBAYASHI:

"Out of the question"? So you believe it couldn't have been true.

IRIS CHANG:

Hmm.

KOBAYASHI:

Let's not mince words. It was a fake. You invented it.

IRIS CHANG:

Well, there was a lot of hearsay, there were a lot of groundless rumors. Naturally.

KOBAYASHI:

Naturally, there were groundless rumors.

IRIS CHANG:

I was fooled into believing in one of them.

KOBAYASHI:

You admit that you were "fooled into believing it"?

IRIS CHANG:

I can't say that sort of thing didn't happen. It did. I think there were a lot of groundless rumors...

KOBAYASHI:

So you were fooled into believing in groundless rumors?

"The more I investigated, the less I knew of the truth"

IRIS CHANG:

Behind the scenes... There were Chinese people who were frightened that something of that sort would happen. There were cases where the Japanese really did those things, and others where the Chinese side deliberately tried to make it look as if the Japanese had done them. I don't really know which was which. The more I investigated, the less I knew.

KOBAYASHI:

The less you knew? OK. I see.

IRIS CHANG:

Hmm... I didn't know what the truth was anymore.

KOBAYASHI:

I see.

AYAORI:

So you endured a barrage of criticisms, had many things pointed out to you, and as a result you opened a fresh investigation?

IRIS CHANG:

Exactly. I investigated a wide range of things. I looked into a wide variety of matters relating to World War II. I studied widely about the battles of the Japanese army. I found that no matter how much I investigated, the materials were inconclusive.

AYAORI:

Yes, that's true, isn't it?

IRIS CHANG:

Yes. It became increasingly agonizing. I couldn't retract my book, not after it had become a bestseller.

AYAORI:

Did you start to wish you could retract it?

IRIS CHANG:

Oh, no. Things had gone too far for that. I'd made a reputation for myself.

KOBAYASHI:

So you're saying, "what's done is done." You admit that you were fooled into believing certain things.

IRIS CHANG:

But thankfully, the Japanese government admitted the incident.

KOBAYASHI:

Yes, it did. But let's leave that subject for another time.

The truth is that the Japanese army
Restored public order in Nanking in six weeks

KOBAYASHI:

Photos taken two days after the Japanese army marched into Nanking show Japanese soldiers tenderly holding Chinese babies, tending fires to warm them, and so on. There are plenty of such photos, so I'm sure you must have seen them [see Figure 9]. It must have seemed to you that there was something odd about the story China was telling.

Figure 9.
A photograph of the city life of Nanking, taken on December 17, 1937. This photo was taken four days after the Japanese army occupied Nanking. The photo shows people getting a haircut, as well as a child smiling; you can see that the people of China are on their way to restoring their everyday life [photo printed in *Asahi Graph* magazine. Published January 12, 1938, by *Asahi Shimbun*].

IRIS CHANG:

Hmm. I wrote that the Japanese army killed 350,000 people in six weeks. But I started to wonder whether the truth was that the Japanese had completely restored public order to Nanking in six weeks.

AYAORI:

You understood that much by then.

KOBAYASHI:

You recognized that.

IRIS CHANG:

Considering that they had restored order soon after the entering, I realized that such incidents were in fact quite rare.

KOBAYASHI:

Yes. The records show that, by about December 20, order had been completely restored in Nanking. You must have been taken aback when you investigated that aspect.

IRIS CHANG:

Starting with the problem of the fake photos, well, I don't believe there was no fighting at all, but the Chinese were not fighting as soldiers. They fought in the guise of civilians or as so-called "guerrillas."

KOBAYASHI:
Soldiers dressed as civilians.

IRIS CHANG:
Right. So the Japanese army was engaged in mopping up pockets of soldiers in plain clothes who were shooting at them. To some observers that would have looked like the Japanese were massacring civilians, but in fact Chinese soldiers were attacking while disguised as civilians. I'm sure the numbers of people killed were not that great. I think the Japanese managed to mop up the guerrillas.

KOBAYASHI:
No, I don't think the numbers were so high. Investigation by us indicates that about 200 soldiers dressed as civilians were shot dead.

IRIS CHANG:
Maybe it was around there. That's probably correct, but the Chinese knew that if they wore military uniforms they would be shot dead, so they dressed as civilians when they came after the Japanese.

The Americans experienced the same thing during the

Vietnam War. They couldn't tell between a farmer and a soldier, so they sprayed defoliant across agricultural areas, killing many people. They dropped incendiary bombs. They burned them with napalm bombs. It was the same sort of thing as what the Americans experienced. That is, they couldn't tell between a civilian and a soldier.

AYAORI:
The situation was the same in the Iraq War.

KOBAYASHI:
That's right. Incidentally, for our readers' reference, engaging in combat while out of uniform was forbidden under international law in times of war. This was because, at the time, it was decided among all nations, in treaties under international law, that anyone who broke this rule could be shot.

IRIS CHANG:
Well, China is the land of *The Water Margin.** It was a place where there was no clear distinction between soldiers and civilians. What mattered was winning, no matter how you got the job done.

---

*An ancient Chinese novel during the Ming Dynasty. A story of former bureaucrats and different class of people forming an organization to fight against the government forces.

"It hurt my conscience to continue writing"

KOBAYASHI:

So if I may summarize, when you investigated later, you found that there were a lot of problems with your book. Photographs had been faked or were from different archives. So you realized that you had been made to seize upon those materials.

IRIS CHANG:

It really struck me that I'd been misled when I realized that I had relied too heavily on the material provided by anti-Japanese groups of China and had written too much from their point of view, yet I'd sold 500,000 copies of my book and couldn't retract it. After that it started to hurt my conscience to continue writing as a writer or a journalist.

OIKAWA:

Did the people who manipulated you into writing this book notice that you were harboring suspicions about it?

IRIS CHANG:

Hmm. I think they were trying to use me as a billboard. But as the criticisms from Japan were so fierce, I couldn't bear it on my own.

5

I Was Used by
The United States to Bash Japan

Who would be troubled if Iris Chang
Became aware of the truth?

OIKAWA:

But if you had let it be known that you thought the things you had written might be wrong, it could be troublesome to those who led you to write them.

IRIS CHANG:

Yes, I think so. Probably.

OIKAWA:

Who would be troubled the most?

IRIS CHANG:

Hmm.

OIKAWA:

When you began to realize just how wrong your original information was and just how mistaken your writings were, who was troubled by that? The United States or China?

IRIS CHANG:

The first book review appeared in an American newspaper. It exposed that the reviewer was an American who had a Chinese wife. It started to reveal just how incredibly organized the operation was.

So I didn't know the full story of what kind of fight I was in, but I resolved to track it down.

OIKAWA:

Didn't you know? Your book was on *The New York Times* Bestseller List for the longest time.

IRIS CHANG:

Oh, yes. *The New York Times*, that's right. I think the Times was very cooperative in the early days. But when it became exposed to me that China was pulling the strings, my position started to feel a bit dicey.

AYAORI:

Their main source comes from China's lobbying activities. But as you mentioned earlier, the United States had come to change their historical perspective. So were both China and the United States involved?

IRIS CHANG:

Yes. I guess there were things they wanted to use.

China wanted to increase its trade with the United States. It also wanted to expand its military. Then the "Japan-passing" episode occurred during the Clinton administration.

AYAORI:
Yes, that's right.

IRIS CHANG:
Not "Japan-bashing." "Japan-*passing*." A movement started in the United States to bypass Japan and partner with China. That would have been an enormous boon for China.

In other words, I think the idea was to form an alliance with and cozy up to China. The premise was, "We both fought against Japan. We're in the right." But that plan was reversed somewhat under the following Republican administration.

AYAORI:
Yes.

IRIS CHANG:
On the question of whether my conclusions as a journalist were based on facts, I know this will be judged in the courtroom of history. If they were based on facts, that

would be fine. If they were not, I could be put into a tough situation.

KOBAYASHI:
Tough, yes.

"The Bataan Death March could not be avoided"

KOBAYASHI:
I suppose you must have felt that especially keenly when you began gathering information for your fourth book, which was on the Bataan Death March [see Figure 10], an event about American soldiers in the Philippines. For

Figure 10.
The Bataan Death March is a forcible transfer by the Japanese Army of 60,000 – 80,000 Filipino and American prisoners of war after the Battle of Bataan in the Philippines during World War II. What actually happened, however, was that the number of prisoners far surpassed the number that the Japanese army had expected. And since there were not enough trucks to transport all the prisoners, they had no choice but to travel by foot.

example, you probably gained a feeling of how difficult it is to confirm evidence and gather things like photos that can be used as evidence. Things didn't go like *The Rape of Nanking*, so maybe you felt that you had come to a standstill in the middle of your work.

IRIS CHANG:

As I listened to the story, I thought that the Japanese had horrifically abused the prisoners and committed something like the Holocaust. But as I investigated, I got the feeling that the soldiers' misfortune could not be avoided.

The Japanese were in the same position. The Japanese also had nothing to eat and were escaping in fear for their lives.

KOBAYASHI:

That's right. The captured American soldiers could walk easily, as they had only a single canteen to carry, whereas the Japanese soldiers had to carry a full pack of arms weighing 40kg. They were walking in a line with the prisoners, along the same road, huffing and puffing with exertion.

IRIS CHANG:

Yes, they were. I realized that the people who said they were abused by the Japanese army counted being fed Japanese food as "abuse." The Japanese eat burdock, but the English soldiers thought being fed tree roots was terribly cruel. I realized that there were misunderstandings like that.

Similarly, there were many stories of people dying from the scorching heat, but that was because there were no vehicles to transport them.

"The more I investigated, the more I realized That things were fabricated"

KOBAYASHI:

I gather from what you're saying that, when you investigated, you became suspicious that the photos you were given were too convenient for the book, or seemed to drop into your hands too easily.

IRIS CHANG:

There was also the problem of interpreting documents. I investigated them, but...

Going back to our earlier discussion of Nanking, there were real reports in a Japanese newspaper at the time about "competitions to kill 100 people with one sword" and so forth. I took these as documentary evidence and drew on them, but, how shall I put this... I came to understand that these stories weren't true, either. They were published to stir up people's fighting spirit.

I learned that it wasn't possible to kill a hundred people with one Japanese sword as Shichihei Yamamoto* suggested. I didn't know that. In sword-fighting movies, it looked like you could kill any number of people with a single sword, so I thought something like that had happened.

The Japanese force that entered Nanking probably numbered around 50,000. In my book I wrote that 50,000 Japanese soldiers had killed 350,000 people with their swords. Then I said they shot them with machine guns, but the Japanese were short of ammunition. They couldn't afford to waste bullets.

KOBAYASHI:

That's right, they didn't shoot. So based on what you wrote, for example, "they shot them with machine guns," since I don't think you made up the whole story from scratch, you might have taken your cue from

---

* Shichihei Yamamoto (1921-1991): A publication manager and a critic in the post-war period. He had opened his original Japanese civilization theory through his works such as *The Japanese and the Jews*.

somewhere. This suggests that you may have been provided with fake documents.

IRIS CHANG:
Hmm…

KOBAYASHI:
So actually, even those things didn't exist, right? Did you just write what you were told to write?

IRIS CHANG:
Hmm. Shooting with machine guns was the American military's practice, when they were killing Japanese people on the southern front.

KOBAYASHI:
That's right.

IRIS CHANG:
Crossfire was a technique used by the Americans. I wrote that the Japanese army did that, but in fact the Japanese army didn't have that kind of firepower.

KOBAYASHI:
No, they didn't, it's just as you say.

IRIS CHANG:

Generally all soldiers were armed with things like bayonets. But it's hard to see how they could have killed so many people that way.

6

The Truth Behind the Made-up Estimate of 300,000 people

"I was used because I was the type of person Who would be popular among Americans"

KOBAYASHI:

In regard to the composition of the story, based on what you've said, it seems like there was an editor for the book. Was there actually a person in charge of editing the book?

I have also done some editing work before, and from hearing what you said just now, it seems as if you had an editor overseeing various aspects of the story's plot, such as the incorporation of the American-style use of machine guns. Is that right?

IRIS CHANG:
Hmm…

KOBAYASHI:
So you had someone serving as a sort of navigator?

IRIS CHANG:
Hmm, I was young and ambitious, and was driven by a sense of justice, so I was shocked that such a major incident had been covered up. I thought, "This has been covered up due to the Cold War," so I had a burning sense of justice. I felt that I must let the world know about this incident, but gradually I started being attacked in various ways and certain parts of my story began to fall apart.

KOBAYASHI:
Who taught you these types of assumptions regarding your perspective of history? How did you acquire such a historical perspective?

IRIS CHANG:
I feel as though I was targeted and used.

KOBAYASHI:
I see.

AYAORI:
You were targeted by a Chinese lobbyist group?

IRIS CHANG:

Hmm, yes. I was the type of person who would be popular among Americans.

KOBAYASHI:

That seems to be true, looking at your photos and so on.

IRIS CHANG:

I was tall, had long hair, and was attractive…

KOBAYASHI:

Yes, you seemed a little bit like an actress…

IRIS CHANG:

I was the kind of person who would be very popular among Americans, and I was also targeted because I could write.

"People gathered the data for me, And I simply compiled it into a book"

AYAORI:

Did you write the entire book by yourself, or…?

IRIS CHANG:

I was aiming to work as a journalist for my profession, so I feel that I was responsible for the text…

OIKAWA:

There wasn't a ghostwriter?

IRIS CHANG:

Well, various materials had been collected.

KOBAYASHI:

So that means, in terms of editing, there were research assistants…

IRIS CHANG:

I wrote the book as a representative…

AYAORI:

You wrote it as a representative?

KOBAYASHI:

There were actually some people who wrote the individual parts for you?

IRIS CHANG:

Yes, that's what I mean when I say I wrote the book as a representative.

AYAORI:

Did several people write the book together? Were several people involved in writing it?

IRIS CHANG:
That's a bit hard to say… It is true that many portions were gathered as data [see Figure 11]…

KOBAYASHI:
So parts were gathered.

IRIS CHANG:
The truth is that I just had to put them together…

KOBAYASHI:
I see.

AYAORI:
So you put them together into a book? That was your role?

Figure 11.
This photo was originally printed in the November 10, 1937 issue of a Japanese magazine, *Asahi Graph*. It shows women and children, escorted by Japanese soldiers, happily returning home from farm work. However, in *The Rape of Nanking*, the big smile on the children and the soldier in this picture were modified and made unclear, and the caption, "The Japanese rounded up thousands of women. Most of them were gang raped or forced into military prostitution" was added. This is also an example of the data, gathered for the book, which distorted the fact.

KOBAYASHI:

It seems like what you are saying is that the primary manuscript of the book, in other words... the various parts of the primary manuscript were prepared for you by those "research assistants"...

IRIS CHANG:

Many portions had been completed so that I could write the sections right away...

AYAORI:

After you wrote the book, did someone make adjustments to it?

IRIS CHANG:

Ugh.

AYAORI:

Was the manuscript published exactly as you wrote it, or were some parts changed?

IRIS CHANG:

Ugh... Please let me go now...

KOBAYASHI:

No, we have to continue.

The figure "300,000 people" was based on The numbers of people who died in The Great Tokyo Air Raids and atomic bombings

KOBAYASHI:

This book had various points of controversy, and it seems that the most significant ones are: the number of people dead being placed at "over 300,000," and the number of people raped being placed at "between 20,000 and 80,000." These two figures appear to be the two central pillars of the story.

IRIS CHANG:

Oh… [*Sighs.*]

KOBAYASHI:

Did the final manuscript that you initially compiled use these expressions? Were these the figures that you stated?

IRIS CHANG:

Well… Actually some people tried hard to get me to increase the number to 300,000…

AYAORI:

You were asked to increase the number?

KOBAYASHI:

Is that what the editor told you to do?

IRIS CHANG:

It seems the numbers were 100,000 for the Great Tokyo Air Raids, 140,000 for Hiroshima [see Figure 12], and 70,000 for Nagasaki. Around 300,000 Japanese people had died, so the number "300,000" was insisted upon.

KOBAYASHI:

Specifically speaking, who said that to you directly?

IRIS CHANG:
Well...

KOBAYASHI:

Who made that request?

Figure 12.
The burnt out city after the Great Tokyo Air Raids in March 1945 (left).
Hiroshima city burnt out after the Atomic bombing in August 1945 (right).

IRIS CHANG:
A variety of people were involved in the publishing of the book…

KOBAYASHI:
Well…

OIKAWA:
Was it the U.S. publishing company, or its editors?

IRIS CHANG:
Well, they requested a number around there, because…

OIKAWA:
So it was the publishing company that said that.

IRIS CHANG:
If, for example, I'd said 20,000 or 10,000, the book probably wouldn't have sold very well. So I was told that I had to put the number at that level because of the desire to make the book sensational…

KOBAYASHI:
So you were told to put the number at around 300,000, in some way or another…

IRIS CHANG:

They wanted at least 300,000. I think it would've been better if the number was higher.

AYAORI:

Was it the publishing company who wanted that, or was it the GA?

IRIS CHANG:

I can't say. I am the writer, so it's my responsibility, and not the publishing company's. That's what I believe. But the idea that it was done over a period of six weeks is just awful. Converting this to one year, one year is 52 weeks, so multiplied by 10, the number becomes about 3 million.

This means that Japanese people carried out violence in which the number of Japanese people who died in all of World War II, would have been killed in a single year.

KOBAYASHI:

So you're saying that the number was calculated by working it out backwards.

IRIS CHANG:

Well, this would indicate that the Japanese are crueler than the Americans. I think the intention was to say that the United States had no choice but to participate in the war because Japan was killing people in this manner.

If the number had only been "200," there wouldn't be any point to publishing the book.

7

"I Was Drugged and Led To Commit Suicide"

"Maybe even the hospital was involved"

AYAORI:

When you started to learn about the actual circumstances of the Nanking Incident, did you speak to anyone about this? Did you tell anyone that the reality didn't seem to match the content of the book?

IRIS CHANG:

Well... [*Sighs*.] I had become a star, so it was very difficult... I had received a number of work requests and was interacting with a variety of people. And in the middle of all that, I sometimes revealed my doubts about the content.

AYAORI:

As a result of this, with whom did your relationships get sour in particular?

IRIS CHANG:

Hmm...

KOBAYASHI:

This is a courtroom before God. Either you speak here or, though I'm not sure if you are familiar with the wrathful god Yama,[*] you will be made to confess before Yama at some time. Either way, you must experience one of these processes somewhere.

IRIS CHANG:

[*Sniffles and begins to cry.*]

KOBAYASHI:

Please be honest with us here.

IRIS CHANG:

Well... I feel that maybe even the hospital was involved...

AYAORI:

You were hospitalized several times.

---

[*] The King of Hell who is said to give judgment on the sins of the dead.

IRIS CHANG:

Hmm. I think that maybe I was being given too much medication by my doctor…

AYAORI:

I see…

IRIS CHANG:

The doctor said that I had some type of psychological abnormality, so I had to take some medicine. I think I was being given too much medication. After that, I believe that maybe they did me in and made it look as if I had spontaneously committed suicide…

KOBAYASHI:

Oh, I see.

"Sometimes I felt as if I was being followed"

OIKAWA:

It is said that you were experiencing depression. Is this true?

IRIS CHANG:

Hmm. I think my symptoms were close to that, but I'm not sure if this happened on its own. I think that perhaps the hospital was involved…

KOBAYASHI:
I see.

IRIS CHANG:
If the hospital was involved, I think this means that the CIA could have been involved.

KOBAYASHI:
Were you admitted into a hospital on the west coast?

IRIS CHANG:
Hmm…

KOBAYASHI:
Or maybe it was "that" hospital on the east coast?

IRIS CHANG:
Well… It seems as if they were communicating with each other. I was referred to a hospital, and it seems like various things like this were happening…

AYAORI:
Who referred you to the hospital?

IRIS CHANG:

I don't know… I can't…

AYAORI:

You don't know?

IRIS CHANG:

Well, it is true that I wasn't able to sleep.

AYAORI:

You couldn't sleep?

IRIS CHANG:

But…

AYAORI:

You were referred to a hospital…

IRIS CHANG:

Sometimes I felt as if I was being followed. I would constantly change my address and stay at hotels. I started to feel that I had to do various things like this to stay safe. When I said that I felt as if I was being followed, I was told by my doctor that I was showing hallucinogenic symptoms. I was told various things like I should take mood-stabilizing medications. I'm not really sure what happened.

KOBAYASHI:
In other words, you're saying that the hospital or your doctor was also part of what you thought was a conspiracy?

IRIS CHANG:
Friendly and supportive people were making various arrangements for me...

AYAORI:
Supportive people...

IRIS CHANG:
I trusted them.

"If I were still alive and were to hold a press Conference, that would cause problems for them"

AYAORI:
You implied earlier that you were killed. Does this mean that, in the end, you were led into taking medications and committing suicide?

IRIS CHANG:
I was said to be depressed, but I don't really think that this is true. Maybe...

KOBAYASHI:
Exactly what do you mean by that?

IRIS CHANG:
I feel that maybe I was made sick and made to look as if I had committed suicide. This is probably because if I were still alive and were to hold a press conference denying the authenticity of the book, it would cause problems.

AYAORI:
I see.

IRIS CHANG:
I think that I was silenced and, prior to that, they made an effort to show that I had a psychological abnormality and what I said couldn't be trusted—that the book I wrote when I was still normal is true, but nothing I said later on could be believed.

I don't know if this was done by the United States government or by a Chinese network set up in the United States...

8

The Hidden Background to the book, *The Rape of Nanking*

"In those days, the potential enemy of The United States was Japan"

KOBAYASHI:

Leaving the top-level mastermind aside, if the doctors were involved in such an organized manner, taking into consideration various cases that happened in the past, it appears—objectively speaking—that the United States government was involved because it changed its policy along the way, and it would have been bad if information prior to this change got out.

IRIS CHANG:

Hmm... For the United States, the potential enemy after the collapse of the Soviet Union was Japan.

KOBAYASHI:

Yes.

IRIS CHANG:

And as a result of terrorist attacks, this potential enemy

has changed to Islam. The potential enemy had started to change to Iraq and the entire Islamic world. I think the United States is starting to suspect that China is somehow supporting the Islamic world, supplying Islamic extremists with weapons and missiles via North Korea.

KOBAYASHI:

I see. That's right.

IRIS CHANG:

I researched and wrote about China's missile development, so I know a lot about this. China was supplying technologies to North Korea, and these technologies were undoubtedly being exported from North Korea to the Islamic world.

KOBAYASHI:

Yes, they were.

IRIS CHANG:

I think that missiles were a source of income for North Korean trade, and these weapons of mass destruction were stored in places like Iraq. If these were the situations that led to the Iraq War, things should have turned around.

AYAORI:

Were you taking an anti-Chinese stance, not only regarding historical issues, but also regarding security and military aspects?

IRIS CHANG:

I didn't really know.

AYAORI:

I see. You didn't know.

"Japan is being blamed for the damages From China's civil war"

IRIS CHANG:

I think China is still saying that Japan carried out the Nanking Incident.

AYAORI:

Yes, it is.

IRIS CHANG:

I think China is still saying that anti-Japanese war is the symbol of Chinese unification. But China seems to be placing a lot of blame on Japan regarding its civil war. I'm not a historian, so I'm not really sure, but as a historical researcher I found that an effort was being made to put all of the responsibility on Japan for the damages that were incurred when the army of the Communist Party and Chiang Kai-shek's army were killing each other in great numbers.

AYAORI:
That's true.

KOBAYASHI:
You found it. Indeed…

IRIS CHANG:
I felt what I wrote might be wrong. Also, after looking at the incredible numbers of people who died in communist countries later on such as 20 million and 40 million in events like the large-scale purges by Mao Zedong and the Great Purge in the Soviet Union, it became hard for me to believe that Japan was really such a horrible country.

KOBAYASHI:
I see. The photos of atrocities that you mentioned to us earlier are actually all from the Chinese civil war or the likes of it. For example, it has been fully revealed that the heads are of political criminals of the Communist Party and members of marauding bands. Seeing things

like this, you came to feel that something was wrong...

IRIS CHANG:
Yes. In China's history, there are countless instances of 100,000 or 200,000 people being killed. I don't think, in reality, such things are true of Japanese people...

KOBAYASHI:
I see.

"Rape was actually a serious domestic issue In the United States"

IRIS CHANG:
This may be a bit startling, but the issue of rape actually has to do with the United States. At that time, rape was a serious problem within the United States, so we jumped on the bandwagon. In Japan, incidents of rape don't occur very often.

AYAORI:
Even if such incidents did occur, punishments would be issued in a distinct manner.

KOBAYASHI:
Generally, the title of a book is decided by the editors

and, according to what you just said, it seems that there were instructions from the editors to focus on the matter of rape.

IRIS CHANG:
In the United States, rape was being focused on extensively as a human rights issue...

KOBAYASHI:
So the idea was that if the book had rape as its theme, it would sell well.

IRIS CHANG:
This has become a particularly strong issue under the Democratic administration. Hillary Clinton has been especially vocal regarding the issue of rape.

During the war, as a part of the propaganda of the United States military, a great effort was made to make Japanese people seem like beasts and, since rape was something intolerable, the book was tied in with this...

I think that maybe Mrs. Clinton still believes that there were several hundred thousand sex slaves. There were slaves in the United States and this is viewed harshly, so perhaps these two issues are overlapping each other in her mind.

"The Japanese military was working To prevent rape"

AYAORI:

Did you also research the issue of comfort women?

IRIS CHANG:

Hmm… There is a lack of evidence regarding this as well. It is a strange claim.

AYAORI:

I see.

IRIS CHANG:

It is strange. The United States military has been the one conducting many such acts.

KOBAYASHI:

Yes. That's right.

IRIS CHANG:

It seems that many more Japanese women were raped by the United States military.

KOBAYASHI:

Immediately after the war, there were over 200 cases in a single month in Yokohama City alone.

IRIS CHANG:

Yes. That is appalling. It seems that the places that were occupied by the Japanese army were a bit more orderly in that regard, so it is strange.

KOBAYASHI:

That is your understanding, right?

AYAORI:

Actually, the Japanese military was carrying out measures to prevent such incidents.

IRIS CHANG:

I am aware that there were places like brothels. Basically, in the case of the Japanese military, an effort was made to prevent rape-type assaults on women... It's very hard to say this, but the military was distributing contraceptives. If this was the case, I don't think it would have been possible for rapes to occur.

KOBAYASHI:

Yes, I agree.

IRIS CHANG:

Rapes could not happen. I don't think it was actually possible for such things to happen outside of the brothel facilities.

Therefore, I started to realize that it is somewhat difficult to believe that Japanese troops in Nanking assaulted and committed rape against tens of thousands of women.

KOBAYASHI:
You realized that?

IRIS CHANG:
Yes…

9

The Reality Seen By Iris Chang After Her Death

"Making it look like a suicide by gun Was the work of a professional killer"

AYAORI:
You became depressed, admitted into a hospital and were to a certain degree controlled with medications. In the end, you were shot in the head with a gun. Was this done by another person, or did you commit suicide in this manner? Which is it?

IRIS CHANG:

Well… Making it look like suicide… The United States is a gun society. It's easy to…

KOBAYASHI:

I would like to ask you about this in a straightforward way. It is said that you committed suicide by shooting yourself in the head in the morning, inside a car that was parked on a national highway in the suburbs. Was the location where you were shot inside of a car?

IRIS CHANG:

I don't know. I don't remember. All of a sudden… I died all of a sudden, so I don't know…

KOBAYASHI:

Was it inside your home, inside a hospital or somewhere else?

IRIS CHANG:

I don't really know. I'm not sure. I think it might have been inside my home.

KOBAYASHI:

I see. So it was inside your home.

AYAORI:

If you were suddenly shot as you say, does this mean you did not do the shooting yourself?

IRIS CHANG:

Hmm... But I think my fingerprints were left on the gun. This was the work of a professional killer.

KOBAYASHI:

It was the work of a professional killer? And you say this was in your home?

IRIS CHANG:

Maybe. I don't know who did it... but...

AYAORI:

I see.

IRIS CHANG:

Yes, it is a bit frustrating. I can't help but think that, in the end, I was silenced.

AYAORI:

Yes, I understand.

IRIS CHANG:

It would've been more honorable for me if I'd been killed

by a Japanese ninja—if I'd clearly been stabbed in the back with a Japanese sword...

AYAORI:
A Japanese person would not do such a thing.

KOBAYASHI:
Yes, that would be a tale of heroism, but that's not what happened...

IRIS CHANG:
Hmm...

"The hell in Nanking's spirit world
Was formed due to domestic Chinese purges"

AYAORI:
It has been 10 years now since your death...

IRIS CHANG:
It's been that long?

AYAORI:
Yes.

IRIS CHANG:
Oh, I see.

AYAORI:

Have you been alone this whole time? Or have you been roaming in this world?

IRIS CHANG:

I think my soul has been floating around Nanking and various places…

AYAORI:

Really? You went to Nanking?

IRIS CHANG:

I went to gather information from Nanking's spirit world.

AYAORI:

You visited Nanking's spirit world?

KOBAYASHI:

How was it?

IRIS CHANG:

Actually, there were far more spirits of Chinese people who were killed after World War II, so it was difficult to find spirits who had been killed in Nanking.

KOBAYASHI:

It was difficult?

IRIS CHANG:

Yes, it was actually difficult…

AYAORI:

More people were killed in the Cultural Revolution and purges like that?

IRIS CHANG:

There are many spirits of Chinese people who were killed due to various things. Tens of millions… There actually is a hell.

KOBAYASHI:

There is? OK.

IRIS CHANG:

That's why it was very difficult to check if they had been killed by Japanese troops in Nanking.

KOBAYASHI:

It seems that you went to conduct interviews in the spirit world, but couldn't find the people that you were looking for.

IRIS CHANG:

Hmm… It was extremely difficult.

"I hear many voices accusing me"

AYAORI:

So you have been gathering various information for the past 10 years?

IRIS CHANG:

Yes, and I feel like I'm also running around nightmarish war zones. Or I feel like I'm being hounded by someone in the United States. It seems like I'm running from place to place in the United States. Various things like those.

In the case of the United States, I often have nightmares in which it seems like I'm involved in something like mafia wars and being targeted with guns. When I go to China, there is something like a hell of war and I also gather information there, but it seems like things somehow don't make sense.

Also, after seeing the destruction of the World Trade Center in which 3,000 people died, I lost track of what is what, and I'm no longer sure about what justice is anymore.

AYAORI:

During this time, has anyone given you any words of guidance?

IRIS CHANG:

No, but I hear many voices accusing me.

AYAORI:

Voices accusing you?

IRIS CHANG:

Yes, I hear many of them. I hear many voices accusing me, but guidance, guidance, voices of guidance…

"I was praised by Deng Xiaoping In the spirit world"

KOBAYASHI:

Did you speak with anyone?

IRIS CHANG:

Yes, I think I met Deng Xiaoping.

AYAORI:

Deng Xiaoping… That must have been in the place called Hell.

KOBAYASHI:

What did Deng Xiaoping say?

IRIS CHANG:
I think he shook my hand.

KOBAYASHI:
He shook your hand?

IRIS CHANG:
Hmm...

AYAORI:
Did it seem like he was telling you, "good job" regarding your book?

IRIS CHANG:
I think I was praised for doing a good job of fighting in the united front against Japan.

KOBAYASHI:
I see. I believe Deng Xiaoping was the main culprit behind the incident at Tiananmen Square.

IRIS CHANG:
At that time, I didn't realize that my saying China underwent the incident at Nanking would serve as a replacement for the incident at Tiananmen Square. I didn't really know that. Therefore, surely there are problems now in China.

KOBAYASHI:

As Ayaori just mentioned, according to our spiritual investigation, Deng Xiaoping is in a fairly deep place in Hell.*

IRIS CHANG:

I think that maybe he is a hero in China.

KOBAYASHI:

Yes, in this world, he is.

IRIS CHANG:

Both Deng Xiaoping and I are believed to be heroes.

10

"I Want My Book To be Taken Out of Print"

"I'm still being used by China and South Korea"

AYAORI:

Today you have summarized what you did in your career.

---

*See Ryuho Okawa, *Adam Smith Reigen Ni Yoru "Shin Kokufuron"* [A New Theory of the Wealth of Nations from the Spirit of Adam Smith] (Tokyo: IRH Press, 2010).

You have probably discovered many things during these 10 years, but you are still in an extremely painful situation right now, wandering around the physical world and experiencing some places in the spirit world. However, I think criticisms from people will ease up to some extent when the content of today's session gets published in a book.

IRIS CHANG:
Hmmm... I wonder. Right now China and South Korea are still forming national policies along the lines of what I said and accusing Japan, right? They are using the Nanking Massacre to restrict Japan's right to self-defense and aiming for a hegemony, yes? So if they continue using me, I don't think it's that easy...

AYAORI:
At the very least, if you were to come out and say, "This book should not be used," then the level of your suffering might change.

IRIS CHANG:
I can't rest in peace unless this book is taken out of print.

KOBAYASHI:
I see.

IRIS CHANG:

I was used. However you look at it, I was used, so...

If the situation stands and China winds up using this... in other words, if they use it as grounds to invade Japan and other Asian countries, then "my sin" will become something very heavy indeed, and that would be horrible for me.

I would be saved if you take the book [*The Rape of Nanking*] to be a fraud. But the fact that it is still being used after all this time... it's just... And there are also lots of Americans who believe it to be true.

This has become a source of information, and as such Japan is said to have committed horrific deeds. But if, in the fight against the militia to force the surrender of Nanking, the mere 200 Chinese deaths were reported as a massacre of 300,000 people and rape victims were reported as reaching up into the tens of thousands, if that was nothing more than propaganda, then I cannot take responsibility for a war of hegemony that China is causing in order to expand their military. I simply cannot take that responsibility. I didn't even think it would be used in that way. I only thought I would be able to expose the "evil" of Japan.

China is still broadcasting anti-Japan movies and dramas on television, so I think the brainwashing is still going on.

KOBAYASHI:
Yes, it certainly is.

IRIS CHANG:
But no matter how you look at it, there is no doubt that China is a totalitarian nation. No one is able to criticize the government. And both Hong Kong and Taiwan are facing a crisis as well. Their freedom and democracy are now about to be taken away, and they are starting to be put under centralized control.

Even for Hong Kong, China was saying that the system would remain as it was for 50 more years, but it is already starting to break its promise. I believe that right around the time I put out my book, Hong Kong was being returned, and fifty years haven't even passed by yet, right? I mean, it's only been about ten years, right? But more and more, Hong Kong is moving towards a position of being pressured to follow orders from Beijing, and asset holders are already considering escape.

Organizations like CNN are already in dangerous waters. They can report low-level news regarding the Chinese government, but they are increasingly becoming unable to report important ones. So it is entirely conceivable that they may end up withdrawing from China.

So... I think China is becoming more and more disobedient to the United States.

"Right now, China is trying to rule Japan and the U.S."

OIKAWA:
If you know about it, we would like to hear about what kind of ties that the group Global Alliance for Preserving the History of World War II in Asia has with the United States.

IRIS CHANG:
Umm... What do you mean by "ties"?

OIKAWA:
Is it connected to the U.S. government?

IRIS CHANG:
Umm, well, you see, I think that after World War II, maintaining the UN system enforced through the allied powers was justice. But the Cold War started between

those permanent UN member nations. And after that, we lost the meaning of justice.

Of course, we had justice according to the United States, but the United States itself has started to become shady after the terrorist outbreak. And every time the Democratic and Republican parties switch in power, the standards of justice seem to shift further away from its true meaning.

So, regarding the question of whether the current Japan is right or wrong, the Americans cannot really judge. And there is also the concern that the United States might be positioned under the influence of China within Obama's term of office. So with all of this, there is a chance that what I did was not the right thing to do...

OIKAWA:

Well, what I mean is, are China and the United States getting close in order to bash Japan...

IRIS CHANG:

No, it's more than just having close relations. China is trying to control the United States. It is clear that they are trying to do that right now. They are using the U.S. financial deficit to try to gain control over the United States, right?

And in a similar move, they look at Japan's inability to change its constitution as a weakness and are trying to control Japan through the law, supporting the opposition party in Japan and those kinds of peace activists. In the United States, they are trying to gain control through money and I'm sure they have already started to buy off the U.S. journalism as well.

But you see, I wasn't aware of any of that when I wrote my book. And in terms of investigative reporting, exposing something big is very important to journalists, so... Please, forgive me! I'm so sorry!

I want to apologize to everyone in Japan. My book is a fraud! Please take it out of publication. Don't read it. It is wrong... I'm sorry! I'm so sorry!

KOBAYASHI:
We would also like you to speak to the people in the United States and China, in addition to the Japanese.

11

"There Was No Nanking Massacre"
"I'm Sorry"

"Japan's reputation must be restored; it must"

IRIS CHANG:

Please don't use my book! Please don't use it for ill. There is talk of misusing my book in an effort to register a "Memory of the World," but I don't want this to be registered as a Memory of the World. Please, I beg of you.

Whatever the circumstances, even in the country of "Hakuhatsu san-zen jou,"* you mustn't lie. Lies are wrong.

It is a fact that the atomic bombs were dropped. It is a fact that many people died. It is also a fact that many people were burnt to death by incendiary bombs in the Great Tokyo Air Raids. There is no room for debate regarding those facts. They actually happened.

But this book makes it seem like something that didn't

---

* This literally means, "My white hair extends 3,000 jous (about six miles)". A Chinese poet, Li Bai used these words in his poem to express the depth of his sorrow. This is an example of an exaggerated expression that Chinese people use to express how they feel.

happen at all [the Nanking incident], actually happened. So Japan's honor must be restored; it must.

Yes, it was a war, so of course people did die. But to take it all and use it for some purpose, for propaganda, goes against my conscience as a journalist. So I beg people to stop using this book for anti-Japan purposes, for opposition toward Japan and to justify a Chinese hegemony. This is what I ask. And regarding the fact that some Japanese people have worked hard to criticize my book out of a sense of justice, I am now filled with a deep sense of remorse.

I was practically unknown, and that is why I was targeted. I was young. I wanted to write a book. I wanted to be famous. My ambitions were why I was targeted. And when the book sold well, I was happy. I am not really a deep thinker, so I had absolutely no idea just how much this book would affect global matters! At the time I didn't see that deeply into the issue, but now, I feel that it is very bad that the whole thing has become this much of a major problem.

I cannot agree to contribute to China's attempts at threatening Japan, or to China's efforts to control the Asian region based on a wrong belief that Japan committed atrocities some 80 years ago. That is not right. It's just not right.

I believe it is much better to reshape China into a free and democratic nation that allows the freedom of speech and the freedom of religion.

We will probably see many refugees escaping from China. I want people to know that getting harmed in the past does not allow China to justify itself.

"To the Japanese people: I am so sorry! Please forgive me"

IRIS CHANG:

I never, ever thought for even an instant that a single book like this would have such an impact on the Japanese people, and I am so, so sorry. I am so sorry that my ambition to succeed as a journalist turned into such a heavy burden on you.

Until the kind of democratization and liberation of China that you all want succeed, and until information on things like Deng Xiaoping's evil deeds at Tiananmen is made open to the entire world, my sin will not be forgiven.

I am so sorry! If the people of Japan could forgive me, I would be so relieved. Please forgive me. I am sorry.

I was used. I was young. I didn't know. I'm sorry. I was born after the war, so there is no way I could have known... no way...

AYAORI:
Well, today, you have made an important confession, so...

IRIS CHANG:
I'm sorry. There is no way someone who was born more than 20 years after the war could possibly understand. Just being of Chinese descent doesn't automatically give you that kind of understanding... I mean, you know, there were many, many Japanese people in Shanghai and Nanking during the war who moved out and returned back home to Japan. So, if something that big had actually happened, news about it would have unquestionably found its way into the ears of people all across Japan.

If my book served to make something that didn't happen into something that actually happened, when the Japanese people returning home never even spoke of such a thing, I feel terribly sorry... I am really sorry!

AYAORI:
Well, today we have heard a kind of repentance from you, so...

IRIS CHANG:

Please, please, I beg you to forgive me. I need to hear words of forgiveness... Forgive me. Forgive me.

"Prime Minister Abe isn't the second coming Of Hitler" "Hitler is in China"

KOBAYASHI:

This spiritual message is going to spread, not only throughout Japan but also throughout the United States, China and the entire world. So if you could back us up and give us some support for that, I believe you will be forgiven.

IRIS CHANG:

No, I don't have the power for that. I don't have the power, but I think the democratic activists who are being hounded by China are in touch with you, so please help them.

The United States shouldn't be helping the anti-Japanese groups of China. Instead they should really be helping the activists... I can understand that the U.S. government doesn't want the American people to find out the fact that they recognize their sins of having dropped the atomic bombs and burning Tokyo to the ground. But already, they have committed scores of atrocious acts in the subsequent wars in Vietnam and Iraq... So, it's time for them to swallow their pride and stand on the side of the truth.

Oh, please, God... I beg you to forgive me! I am sorry. I am so sorry.

I have done something horrible to the Americans and Chinese-Americans who believe in my book and act on it; to the Chinese people who are being used by their politicians or, in other words, who are brainwashed; and to the Japanese people who, out of the good of their hearts, keep apologizing, feeling guilt over the evil they believe their forefathers have done. I beg you, please forgive me. I am so sorry!

If the incident I described was actually true, then people would have to face up to it. But that kind of false accusation about something that isn't true just has to be dispelled.

I want people to stop using my book to craft public opinion, to determine national policy or to make judgments on those kinds of legal issues. Please consider it to be a false book.

Your country is being targeted now, too. It is in danger of being taken over. Article 9 of the Japanese Constitution is being seen as a weak spot that leaves you open for an inevitable invasion.

China knows that Japan will not be able to do anything if China delivers a crushing blow to Japan with its first shot. They know that Japan can only counterattack and can never deal the first blow, so I think they will make the first move.

And... what Prime Minister Abe is doing now does not represent the second coming of Hitler in any way. Hitler is in China now. So please, please do not lump me in with that side. I beg you. Cut me loose.

KOBAYASHI:
I understand.

"It is about time that the U.S. Also reflected on itself properly"

IRIS CHANG:
I was killed. So I beg you all to understand that I was manipulated into doing the wrong thing. I want to take this chance to tell all of the Japanese authors,

critics, journalists, and all of the other people who have criticized my book, I want to say to them, "Yes, you were all correct. I am so sorry."

And furthermore, to the writers and journalists who are still using my words for their business, I want to say, "This is all fabricated. It is foolish to think that unreported facts about that time could be discovered in 1997"... Huff, puff [*panting*]... "There are no such thing as facts that come to light some 60 years after the event." I really want people to understand that.

There are many, many Japanese people who moved out of China and returned back home to Japan. There were many witnesses. There were many Japanese people in places like Shanghai and Nanking, and they have all returned home to Japan. So the information is there. If you look for it, you will find it. If you ask, say, 100 people, you should be able to get an almost complete picture of what really happened.

It is not good to say that something happened when it actually didn't.

I think that it is about time that the United States also reflected upon it properly. As for what specifically will happen as a result, that is something that will unfold in the near future, but I think, how should I put it? It's what they chose between two options...

Also, I think they should understand very well that their choice has resulted in causing misfortune. I beg you, please do not use my book as a trigger to start the next war.

KOBAYASHI:

Yes, OK. We would like to understand your message well and spread it. We will tell people of what you said.

IRIS CHANG:

I'm sorry... Well, I suppose China thinks, "dead men tell no tales." But I believe that some people out there will definitely believe in my spiritual message.

KOBAYASHI:

Right.

IRIS CHANG:

I definitely think there are people out there who will believe in it. Unless people see what the real truth was, what the real facts were, they won't be able to discern good from evil.

I want to apologize deeply to all of the honorable

Japanese soldiers I have insulted, and regarding my statement along the lines of, "paying respect to the people enshrined at Yasukuni is like worshiping a bronze statue of Hitler." I want to apologize deeply to all of the souls enshrined there.

I beg your forgiveness. I am sorry.

KOBAYASHI:
Yes, OK.

AYAORI:
I think everyone will understand how you feel.

IRIS CHANG:
Thank you.

KOBAYASHI:
Thank you very much for coming here today.

IRIS CHANG:
I'm very sorry...

12

After Receiving the Spiritual Message From Iris Chang

OKAWA:

[*Claps once.*] Ahh, this is terrible.

Saying, "I didn't think that far" shows that she has been continually exploited. She seemed to have thought that she would lose the power to influence people after her death, but the truth is, the very fact that she is dead has made her an even more convenient tool for anyone to use as much as they want. If she were alive, she could say that her book is wrong. But now she cannot say that anymore.

She clearly stated that she was killed, so we can assume that this was the case. She was most likely killed to be silenced. We should assume that she was used and disposed of.

There is no way that someone who is 12 years younger than me or that Americans could ever know the real truth behind the Nanking incident. How could they know? It's not like there are resources available in English, so you have to have been in Nanking at that time to really understand what happened.

And I think that Mr. Shoichi Watanabe stayed in my dreams from 3:00 in the morning because this issue is probably the very important piece, the starting point. It is as if he wanted to say, "Someone has to remove the root of this issue." No matter how much we make counterarguments, if no one listens then nothing will change. And the Chinese government is still taking the same tone.

However, when dealing with a nation that still cannot tell how many students the military killed in the 1989 Tiananmen Square incident, I simply cannot stop wondering how such a nation could possibly know that the Japanese killed 300,000 people, 80 years ago, and know how many people were raped. This can only be interpreted as pure opportunistic behavior. I should say that they don't deserve the honor of being a first rate country.

For example, they are apparently intimidating Japan by threatening and saying that they are able to shoot down Japanese aircrafts whenever they want. Japan must appear very fragile to them because, even as it debates on this in the Diet, the opposition parties and other parties are siding with China. To China, democratic nations must appear extremely weak and unable to achieve a national consensus. They must feel that they are much, much stronger with their centralized control.

However, neighboring nations and autonomous nations are joining forces for a counterattack, and an encirclement is being formed. It is becoming increasingly clear that it is they [China] who are surrounded.

And South Korea was attempting to form a China-South Korea Alliance. But South Korea is now "sinking,"* and I think it is being made to self-reflect.

I believe that God's wrath will fall in the right places. It would be good if this is manifested by fair means, but if not, we might see much, much more of things like the deluge in Shanghai that has covered the area in water up to the waist.

Ultimately, I will put an end to this issue. I will work hard with that as my goal.

EVERYONE:
Thank you very much.

---

* In April, 2014 South Korean ferry capsized killing around 300 people. The author of this book is comparing the troubles that South Korea is facing to the incident.

Afterword

So, it was just as I thought. I knew that there was no way a Japanese force made up of only 50,000 soldiers could kill over 300,000 civilians in Nanking. After all, Americans were completely fooled and manipulated by China, which is good at making up stories. And the author herself, too, was caught up in such a tragic whirlwind. Iris Chang now seems to be drifting between the Asura Realm of Hell* and the Abysmal Hell.† She may have acted out of her conscience, but her sin is too heavy.

She needs to be forgiven by every Japanese, every American and all of the brainwashed Chinese citizens. But for now, the important issue is not about when her day of salvation will come, but whether or not we can overcome the crisis in Japan and the crisis in Asia. Against a new "Mongol invasion"‡ of Japan, first we must fight an ideological battle. And we must deter the ambition of the "Great Chinese Empire" with the power of liberation and democratization.

> *Ryuho Okawa*
> *Master & CEO of Happy Science Group*
> *June 12, 2014*

---

* A realm of Hell where aggressive and fierceful people fall after death.
† A realm of Hell where people who preached wrong philosophy or religious teachings, and led a lot of people in the wrong direction fall after death.
‡ Given that Xi Jinping is the reincarnation of Genghis Khan, his current expansionist policy can be considered as the equivalent of the Mongol invasions of Japan, which occurred in 1274 and 1281.

About the Author

MASTER RYUHO OKAWA started receiving spiritual messages from Heaven in 1981. Holy beings appeared before him with impassioned messages of urgency, entreating him to deliver God's words to Earth. Within the same year, Master Okawa's deepest subconscious awakened and revealed his calling to become a spiritual leader who is inspiring the world with the power of God's Truths. Through these conversations with divine beings and through profound spiritual contemplation, Master Okawa developed the philosophy that would become the core of his teachings. His communications with Heaven deepened his understanding of God's designs and intentions—how He created our souls, this world, the other world, and the Laws that are the very fabric of the universe.

In 1986, Master Okawa founded Happy Science, a nondenominational universal religion, to share God's

Truths and to help humankind overcome religious and cultural conflicts and usher in an era of peace on Earth. As part of the Happy Science movement, Master Okawa founded a political party, the Happiness Realization Party, as well as a private middle and high school, Happy Science Academy.

The universality and integrity of his spiritual teachings, delivered in his uniquely simple and pragmatic way, have attracted millions of readers and followers in over one hundred countries. In addition to publishing over 1,600 books, Master Okawa has delivered more than 2,200 talks and lectures, and continues to share God's Truths throughout the world.

About Happy Science

In 1986, Master Ryuho Okawa founded Happy Science, a spiritual movement dedicated to bringing greater happiness to humankind by overcoming barriers of race, religion, and culture and by working toward the ideal of a world united in peace and harmony. Supported by followers who live in accordance with Master Okawa's words of enlightened wisdom, Happy Science has grown rapidly since its beginnings in Japan and now extends throughout the world. Today, it has twelve million members around the globe, with faith centers in New York, Los Angeles, San Francisco, Tokyo, London, Sydney, Sao Paulo, and Hong Kong, among many other major cities. Master Okawa speaks at Happy Science centers and travels around the world giving public lectures. Happy Science provides a variety of programs and services to support local communities. These programs include preschools, after-school educational programs for youths, and services for senior citizens and the disabled. Members also participate in social and charitable activities, which in the past have included providing relief aid to earthquake victims in China, New Zealand, and Turkey, and to flood victims in Thailand as well as building schools in Sri Lanka.

Programs and Events

Happy Science faith centers offer regular events, programs, and seminars. Join our meditation sessions, video lectures, study groups, seminars, and book events. Our programs will help you:

- Deepen your understanding of the purpose and meaning of life
- Improve your relationships as you learn how to love unconditionally
- Learn how to calm your mind even on stressful days through the practice of contemplation and meditation
- Learn how to overcome life's challenges
  ...and much more.

International Seminars

Each year, friends from all over the world join our international seminars, held at our faith centers in Japan. Different programs are offered each year and cover a wide variety of topics, including improving relationships, practicing the Eightfold Path to enlightenment, and loving yourself, to name just a few.

Happy Science Monthly

Read Master Okawa's latest lectures in our monthly booklet, Happy Science Monthly. You'll also find stories of members' life-changing experiences, news from Happy Science members around the world, in-depth information about Happy Science movies, book reviews, and much more. Happy Science Monthly is available in English, Portuguese, Chinese, and other languages. Back issues are available upon request. Subscribe by contacting the Happy Science location nearest you.

Contact Information

Happy Science is a worldwide organization with faith centers around the globe. For a comprehensive list of centers, visit the worldwide directory at http://www.happy-science.org or www.happyscience-na.org.

The following are some of the many Happy Science locations:

United States and Canada

New York

79 Franklin Street
New York, NY 10013
Phone: 212-343-7972
Fax: 212-343-7973
Email: ny@happy-science.org
Website: www.happyscience-ny.org

Los Angeles

1590 E. Del Mar Blvd.
Pasadena, CA 91106
Phone: 626-395-7775
Fax: 626-395-7776
Email: la@happy-science.org
Website: www.happyscience-la.org

San Diego

Email: sandiego@happy-science.org

San Francisco

525 Clinton Street
Redwood City, CA 94062
Phone/Fax: 650-363-2777
Email: sf@happy-science.org
Website: www.happyscience-sf.org

Atlanta

1874 Piedmont Ave. NE
Suite 360-C Atlanta, GA 30324
Phone/Fax: 404-892-7770
Email: atlanta@happy-science.org
Website: www.atlanta.happyscience-na.org

Florida

12208 N 56th Street
Temple Terrace, FL 33617
Phone:813-914-7771
Fax: 813-914-7710
Email: florida@happy-science.org
Website: www.happyscience-fl.org

New Jersey

725 River Road, Suite 200
Edgewater, NJ 07025
Phone: 201-313-0127
Fax: 201-313-0120
Email: nj@happy-science.org
Website: www.happyscience-nj.org

Hawaii (Oahu)

1221 Kapiolani Blvd, Suite 920
Honolulu, HI 96814
Phone: 808-591-9772
Fax: 808-591-9776
Email: hi@happy-science.org
Website: www.happyscience-hi.org

Hawaii (Kauai)

4504 Kukui Street
Dragon Building Suite 21
Kapaa, HI 96746
Phone: 808-822-7007
Fax: 808-822-6007
Email: kauai-hi@happy-science.org
Website: www.happyscience-kauai.org

Toronto

323 College Street
Toronto ON M5T 1S2, Canada
Phone/Fax: 1-416-901-3747
Email: toronto@happy-science.org
Website: www.happy-science.ca

Vancouver

#212-2609 East 49th Avenue
Vancouver, V5S 1J9, Canada
Phone: 1-604-437-7735
Fax: 1-604-437-7764
Email: vancouver@happy-science.org
Website: www.happy-science.ca

International

Tokyo
1-6-7 Togoshi, Shinagawa,
Tokyo, 142-0041 Japan
Phone: 81-3-6384-5770
Fax: 81-3-6384-5776
Email: tokyo@happy-science.org
Website: www.happy-science.org

London
3 Margaret Street,
London, W1W 8RE, United Kingdom
Phone: 44-20-7323-9255
Fax: 44-20-7323-9344
Email: eu@happy-science.org
Website: www.happyscience-uk.org

Seoul
162-17 Sadang3-dong,
Dongjak-gu, Seoul, South Korea
Phone: 82-2-3478-8777
Fax: 82-2-3478-9777
Email: korea@happy-science.org
Website: www.happyscience-korea.org

Taipei
No.89, Lane 155,
Dunhua N. Road,
Songshan District,
Taipei City 105, Taiwan
Phone: 886-2-2719-9377
Fax: 886-2-2719-5570
Email: taiwan@happy-science.org
Website: www.happyscience-tw.org

Sydney
516 Pacific Hwy Lane Cove
North,
2066 NSW Australia
Phone: 61-2-9411-2877
Fax: 61-2-9411-2822
Email: aus@happy-science.org
Website: www.happyscience.org.au

Brazil Headquarters
R. Domingos de Morais 1154,
Vila Mariana, Sao Paulo, CEP
04009-002, Brazil
Phone: 55-11-5088-3800
Fax: 55-11-5088-3806
Email: sp@happy-science.org
Website: www.happyscience-br.org

Uganda
Plot 877 Rubaga Road, Kampala,
P.O. Box 34130, Kampala,
Uganda
Phone: 256-78-4728-601
Email:uganda@happy-science.org
Website: www.happyscience-uganda.org

About the Happiness Realization Party

The Happiness Realization Party (HRP) was founded in May 2009 by Master Ryuho Okawa as part of the Happy Science Group to offer concrete and proactive solutions to the current issues such as military threats from North Korea and China and the long-term economic recession. HRP aims to implement drastic reforms of the Japanese government, thereby bringing peace and prosperity to Japan. To accomplish this, HRP proposes two key policies:

1) Strengthening the national security and the Japan-U.S. alliance which plays a vital role in the stability of Asia.
2) Improving the Japanese economy by implementing drastic tax cuts, taking monetary easing measures and creating new major industries.

HRP advocates that Japan should offer a model of a religious nation that allows diverse values and beliefs to coexist, and that contributes to global peace.

For more information, please visit www.hr-party.jp/en.

About IRH Press

IRH Press Co., Ltd, based in Tokyo, was founded in 1987 as a publishing division of Happy Science. IRH Press publishes religious and spiritual books, journals, magazines and also operates broadcast and film production enterprises. For more information, visit OkawaBooks. com.

Other Books by Ryuho Okawa

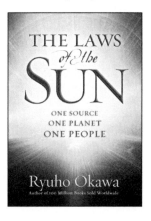

THE LAWS OF THE SUN
One Source, One Planet, One People

ISBN: 978-1-937673-04-8
$24.95 (Hardcover)

IMAGINE IF YOU COULD ASK GOD why He created this world and what spiritual laws He used to shape us—and everything around us. If we could understand His designs and intentions, we could discover what our goals in life should be and whether our actions move us closer to those goals or farther away.

At a young age, a spiritual calling prompted Ryuho Okawa to outline what he innately understood to be universal truths for all humankind. In *The Laws of the Sun*, Okawa outlines these laws of the universe and provides a road map for living one's life with greater purpose and meaning.

In this powerful book, Ryuho Okawa reveals the transcendent nature of consciousness and the secrets of our multidimensional universe and our place in it. By understanding the different stages of love and following the Buddhist Eightfold Path, he believes we can speed up our eternal process of development. *The Laws of the Sun* shows the way to realize true happiness—a happiness that continues from this world through the other.

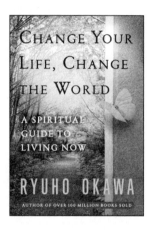

CHANGE YOUR LIFE,
CHANGE THE WORLD
A SPIRITUAL GUIDE TO LIVING NOW

ISBN: 978-0-9826985-0-1
$16.95 (Paperback)

MASTER RYUHO OKAWA calls out to people of all nations to remember their true spiritual roots and to build our planet into a united Earth of peace, prosperity, and happiness. With the spiritual wisdom contained in this book, each and every one of us can change our lives and change the world.

"To save the seven billion people on Earth,
God has countless angels working constantly,
every day, on His behalf." —Chapter 3

THE MOMENT OF TRUTH
BECOME A LIVING ANGEL TODAY

ISBN: 978-0-9826985-7-0
$14.95 (Paperback)

MASTER OKAWA shows that we are essentially spiritual beings and that our true and lasting happiness is not found within the material world but rather in acts of unconditional and selfless love toward the greater world. These pages reveal God's mind, His mercy, and His hope that many of us will become living angels that shine light onto this world.

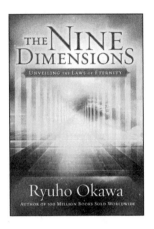

THE NINE DIMENSIONS
UNVEILING THE LAWS OF ETERNITY

ISBN: 978-0-9826985-6-3
$15.95 (Paperback)

THIS BOOK IS YOUR GATE TO HEAVEN. In this book, Master Okawa shows that God designed this world and the vast, wondrous world of our afterlife as a school with many levels through which our souls learn and grow. This book is a window into the mind of our loving God, who encourages us to grow into greater angels.

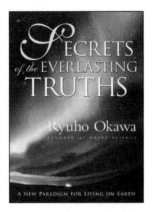

SECRETS OF
THE EVERLASTING TRUTHS
A New Paradigm for Living on Earth

ISBN: 978-1-937673-10-9
$14.95 (Paperback)

OUR BELIEF IN THE INVISIBLE IS OUR FUTURE. It is our knowledge about the everlasting spiritual laws and our belief in the invisible that will make it possible for us to solve the world's problems and bring our entire planet together. When you discover the secrets in this book, your view of yourself and the world will be changed dramatically and forever.

THE LAWS OF PERSEVERANCE
REVERSING YOUR COMMON SENSE

ISBN: 978-1-937673-56-7
$14.95 (Paperback)

"No matter how much you suffer, the Truth will gradually shine forth as you continue to endure hardships. Therefore, simply strengthen your mind and keep making constant efforts in times of endurance, however ordinary they may be.

Eventually, you will come out of your slump and overcome your hardships. And, as you try and aim to reverse the common sense, you will one day understand that people can be "undefeated" even if they seem to have lost in this world. In that process, you may sometimes feel that virtue is being generated."

—From Postscript

THINK BIG!

BE POSITIVE AND BE BRAVE TO ACHIEVE YOUR DREAMS!

ISBN: 978-1-941779-06-4
$14.95 (Paperback)

In *Think Big* Master Ryuho Okawa shares his own philosophy of thinking big, thinking positive, and being brave for they are essential mindsets in achieving our dreams. While there is an especial emphasis on developing this philosophy while we're young, it is universal and valuable for people of all ages and all walks of life who want to achieve their dreams and live a successful life. If you do not have any dreams yet, then this is a must-have book for discovering why having ideals are an essential part of life. If you already have aspirations, then discover how to make them come true. If you are in college, find out valuable tips on how to get a head start on developing the think big mindset.

Also by Ryuho Okawa

THE SCIENCE OF HAPPINESS
10 Principles for Manifesting Your Divine Nature

THE GOLDEN LAWS
History through the Eyes of the Eternal Buddha

THE STARTING POINT OF HAPPINESS
A Practical and Intuitive Guide to Discovering Love, Wisdom, and Faith

LOVE, NURTURE, AND FORGIVE
A Handbook to Add a New Richness to Your Life

AN UNSHAKABLE MIND
How to Overcome Life's Difficulties

THE ORIGIN OF LOVE
On the Beauty of Compassion

INVINCIBLE THINKING
There Is No Such Thing as Defeat

GUIDEPOSTS TO HAPPINESS
Prescriptions for a Wonderful Life

THE LAWS OF HAPPINESS
The Four Principles for a Successful Life

TIPS TO FIND HAPPINESS
Creating a Harmonious Home for Your Spouse, Your Children, and Yourself

THE PHILOSOPHY OF PROGRESS
Higher Thinking for Developing Infinite Prosperity

THE ESSENCE OF BUDDHA
The Path to Enlightenment

THE CHALLENGE OF THE MIND
A Practical Approach to the Essential Buddhist Teaching of Karma

THE CHALLENGE OF ENLIGHTENMENT
Realize Your Inner Potential

THE MANIFESTO OF
THE HAPPINESS REALIZATION PARTY

RYUHO OKAWA: A POLITICAL REVOLUTIONARY
The Originator of Abenomics and Father of the Happiness Realization Party

Higher Education Series

THE NEW IDEA OF A UNIVERSITY
The Groundbreaking Mission of Happy Science University

THE BASIC TEACHINGS OF HAPPY SCIENCE
A Happiness Theory on Truth and Faith

Spiritual Interview Series

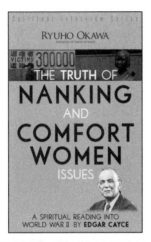

THE TRUTH OF NANKING AND COMFORT WOMEN ISSUES
A Spiritual Reading into World War II
by Edgar Cayce

ISBN: 978-1-937673-86-4
$14.95 (Paperback)

Did the so-called "Nanking Massacre" and the military comfort women forcefully taken by the Japanese troops actually exist as historical facts? In this book, we attempt to investigate whether the two events actually took place by using a new method. This is not merely to restore the international honor of Japan. We are hoping to review the causes of World War II, look over the world justice made by the victorious nations after the war and reveal the true world history.

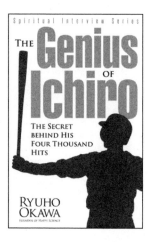

THE GENIUS OF ICHIRO
THE SECRET BEHIND HIS FOUR THOUSAND HITS

ISBN: 978-1-941779-04-0
$14.95 (Paperback)

Ichiro Suzuki arrived in Seattle in 2001 as a mostly anonymous free agent from Japan's NPB, and while there was buzz about his potential, no one really knew what to expect. Since then, he has set many records in American Major League Baseball, including the record for most hits in a single season (262) and longest streak of two-hundred-hit seasons (ten years). On August 21, 2013, he got the four thousandth hit of his professional baseball career. This spiritual interview reveals the "making of Ichiro," including the secrets to his professionalism, his techniques for overcoming slumps, and how he made it to the top. The interview highlights Ichiro's unique traits that continue to impress us, twelve years after he first unleashed the laser beam.

ON HAPPINESS REVOLUTION
A Spiritual Interview with Hannah Arendt

ISBN: 978-1-937673-82-6
$14.95 (Paperback)

Since 2010, Master Ryuho Okawa has published over two hundred spiritual messages, in Japanese, from the spirits of historical men and women and the guardian spirits of today's living figures. With this Spiritual Interview Series, Master Okawa is now making these important messages available in English. The books in this series are messages from the spirits or guardian spirits of people who have a great deal of influence over world affairs. These messages reveal these powerful figures' hidden intentions and disclose facts that even news reporters would have difficulty drawing out. Master Okawa's in-depth analyses of these messages give us the tools that we need to understand and confront the dangers that lie ahead of us. Master Okawa hopes to show readers that the spirit world and spirits are real, and that by understanding spiritual truths, we can bring a peaceful end to international conflicts and create solutions to a variety of global crises.

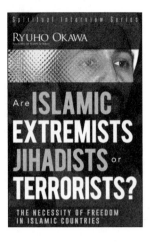

ARE ISLAMIC EXTREMISTS JIHADISTS OR TERRORISTS?

THE NECESSITY OF FREEDOM IN ISLAMIC COUNTRIES

ISBN: 978-1-941779-14-9
$14.95 (Paperback)

The West has been leading a long war on terror since the 9/11 terrorist attacks in 2001 on American soil by Osama bin Laden's al-Qaeda. Even after the assassination of Osama bin Laden on May 2, 2011, by President Obama's Special Forces unit, terrorist attacks have continued around the world. On January 16, 2013, an international crisis erupted when Islamic terrorists organized by Mokhtar Belmokhtar lay siege to an Algerian gas plant. After the Algerian government sent in a special forces unit, thirty-nine foreign hostages were killed and 685 Algerian workers and one hundred foreigners escaped or were freed. ★

Are the attacks by Islamic extremist groups like al-Qaeda and the organization led by Mokhtar Belmokhtar unjust acts of terror? Or are they justified acts of a holy war, as the self-proclaimed jihadists claim? In this interview with Osama bin Laden, Master Ryuho Okawa provides us with his conclusive answer to these questions.

★ "Q&A: Hostage Crisis in Algeria," BBC News, January 21, 2013, http://www.bbc.com/news/world-africa-21056884.

LEADERSHIP SECRETS OF LIU BANG
THE EMPEROR OF CHINA'S HAN DYNASTY
WITH A SURPRISING CONNECTION WITH STEVEN SPIELBERG

ISBN: 978-1-941779-17-0
$14.95 (Paperback)

Liu Bang, also known as Gaozu, began from humble peasant roots and served as a police officer under the Qin dynasty. He rose through the ranks, first receiving control of western China, and eventually becoming the ruler of China as the founder and first emperor of the Han dynasty (206 BCE–220 CE). The histories of kings and rulers often provide valuable lessons about the universal principles that can be applied to today's management, entrepreneurship, and all types of large undertakings. As this spiritual interview has shown, Liu Bang's strengths and achievements are marked by a strong global element. Everyone who aspires to lead a large organization can learn from his ability to win people's hearts. You may be surprised to discover that this long-ago emperor of China is living today in the United States as one of the world's most famous film directors, Steven Spielberg.

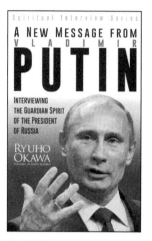

A NEW MESSAGE
FROM VLADIMIR PUTIN
INTERVIEWING THE GUARDIAN SPIRIT
OF THE PRESIDENT OF RUSSIA

ISBN: 978-1-937673-94-9
$14.95 (Paperback)

We hereby bring you the most recent spiritual message from the guardian spirit of President Putin, the politician who is the center of attention of not just the people of Russia but of the whole world, regardless of it being in a good or a bad way. In the Preface, it says, "President Putin's true intentions, which are 90 percent misunderstood."

We hope that, through this book, the reader will come to understand the true thoughts of Mr. Putin which are still undisclosed to the public. And, we hope that the reader will foresee the new world order that this skilled politician is thinking of, and make use of that in predicting how the international affairs will turn out in the future.

THE NEW DIPLOMATIC STRATEGIES OF SIR WINSTON CHURCHILL

A SPIRITUAL INTERVIEW WITH THE FORMER PRIME MINISTER REGARDING THE AGE OF PERSEVERANCE

ISBN: 978-1-937673-85-7

$14.95 (Paperback)

Today, two politicians are criticized and compared to Hitler; President Vladimir Putin of Russia and Prime Minister Shinzo Abe of Japan. Are these politicians really dangerous to be likened to Hitler? Or, just like in Hitler's case, can it be that another truly dangerous politician exists in another country that is yet to be discovered? If there is a chance to hear the opinion of Sir Winston Churchill, considered to be Hitler's arch enemy, journalists around the world would probably be interested to hear this. The series on Spiritual Messages by Ryuho Okawa, Happy Science, made this possible. This book contains a record of an interview conducted with the spirit of former British Prime Minister Churchill by Master Okawa in March this year. It is a record of an interview on issues related to the "next appearance of Hitler," and on current international affairs.

THE ART OF BUSINESS REVITALIZATION

MANAGEMENT WISDOM FROM JACK WELCH,
CARLOS GHOSN, AND BILL GATES

ISBN: 978-1-937673-70-3
$19.95 (Paperback)

In *The Art of Business Revitalization: Management Wisdom from Jack Welch*, Carlos Ghosn, and Bill Gates, Master Ryuho Okawa conducts spiritual interviews with three of the greatest executives of our time. General Electric's Jack Welch, Renault and Nissan's Carlos Ghosn, and Microsoft's Bill Gates give readers a glimpse into how they took hold of opportunities and turned them into successes. What management philosophies helped Jack Welch and Carlos Ghosn turn around their companies during downturns? What is Bill Gates's secret to creating products that become global standards? What human resources management and education philosophies have they drawn upon to keep their companies at the top? This book reveals the secrets to their achievements.

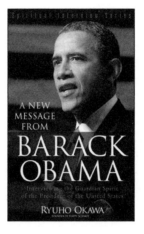

A NEW MESSAGE FROM
BARACK OBAMA
INTERVIEWING THE GUARDIAN SPIRIT OF
THE PRESIDENT OF THE UNITED STATES

ISBN: 978-1-937673-89-5
$14.95 (Paperback)

In April 2014, President Obama embarked on his fifth trip to Asia during his time in office to discuss the pressing issues in the Asia-pacific region. A week before his Asia trip, Master Ryuho Okawa held a spiritual interview with Barack Obama, which revealed his true objectives of his Asia tour and about his thoughts on current affairs in the world. What is President Obama's vision of America's role in the world today? Why does he believe that America is not the world's policeman? This spiritual interview reveals President Obama's stance on international relations including America's relationship with China, the Ukraine crisis and Islamic extremism. It also discloses his honest feelings about Japanese Prime Minister Abe and Russian President Putin. Now that America is "on the verge of crisis," as the guardian spirit of President Obama says in this interview, we all need to think about how we can achieve security, justice and peace in the world without the "world's policeman."

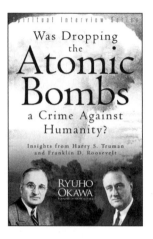

WAS DROPPING THE ATOMIC BOMBS A CRIME AGAINST HUMANITY?

INSIGHTS FROM HARRY S. TRUMAN
AND FRANKLIN D. ROOSEVELT

ISBN: 978-1-937673-78-9
$14.95 (Paperback)

Was there any true justification for the atomic bombing of Hiroshima and Nagasaki? To answer to this question, Master Ryuho Okawa conducted spiritual interviews with Harry S. Truman and Franklin D. Roosevelt, the two presidents who presided over the United States' participation in World War II. Could anything justify the use of nuclear weapons on civilians? Was Pearl Harbor really a sneak attack, or did Franklin Roosevelt know of it beforehand? This book reveals valuable information that will help the world gain a truthful understanding of world history.

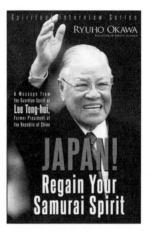

JAPAN! REGAIN YOUR SAMURAI SPIRIT

A MESSAGE FROM THE GUARDIAN SPIRIT OF LEE TENG-HUI,
FORMER PRESIDENT OF THE REPUBLIC OF CHINA

IISBN: 978-1-937673-77-2
$14.95 (Paperback)

This book is the record of interviews conducted on Former President of Taiwan Lee Teng-hui's subconscious [guardian spirit] in February 2014. His true thoughts, as well as the truth on modern East-Asian history, were revealed in these interviews. The book is filled with hints on how to give another thought to the causes of World War II. As it is stated in the afterword, this is a book which we want "all politicians, all people in the media, and everyone who talks about politics" to read.

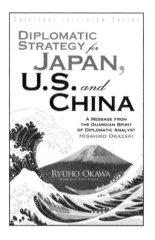

DIPLOMATIC STRATEGY FOR JAPAN, U.S. AND CHINA

A MESSAGE FROM THE GUARDIAN SPIRIT OF DIPLOMATIC ANALYST HISAHIKO OKAZAKI

ISBN: 978-1-937673-75-8
$14.95 (Paperback)

This book contains the interview conducted with the guardian spirit of former diplomat, Hisahiko Okazaki, a conservative commentator representative to Japan. An astonishing relation between Admiral Perry and Okazaki is revealed in this interview. By reading this book, you will come to know what Admiral Perry thinks on the current situation of the world, and the relation between Japan and the United States, 160 years later since he opened up Japan which was in seclusion.

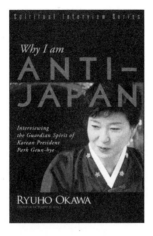

WHY I AM ANTI-JAPAN
INTERVIEWING THE GUARDIAN SPIRIT OF
KOREAN PRESIDENT PARK GEUN-HYE

ISBN: 978-1-937673-67-3
$14.95 (Paperback)

This book is the record of interviews conducted on President Park's subconscious [guardian spirit] in February 2014, which were done in order to find out the fundamental reason to her anti-Japanese sentiments. Her true thoughts, as well as the truth on modern Japan-Korea history, were revealed in these interviews. By having numerous people in the world know of this truth, starting with the Japanese, South Koreans, Americans and the Chinese, the path to create a constructive future of the Pacific Basin should open as we resolve the conflicting emotions between Japan and South Korea in the international society.

A WARNING TO
SOUTH KOREA'S PRESIDENT
WORDS FROM HER FATHER,
FORMER PRESIDENT PARK CHUNG-HEE

ISBN: 978-1-937673-65-9
$14.95 (Paperback)

Park Chung-hee served as the president of the Republic of Korea (South Korea) for almost sixteen years, from 1963 until his death in 1979. Today, people around the world know him as the assassinated father of Park Geun-hye, the current and first female president of South Korea. In this spiritual interview, Park Chung-hee's spirit shares his opinions on the roles of South Korea, Japan, the United States, China, and North Korea in the global context. What are his thoughts on the Takeshima island dispute, the comfort-women issue, China's future prospects, and the direction South Korea should take as a country? A Warning to South Korea's President is a father's message to his daughter as he seeks to guide their nation in the right direction. This interview lets us see history in a new light and shows us how to build a better future for the Asia-Pacific region.

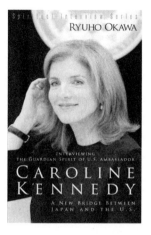

INTERVIEWING THE GUARDIAN SPIRIT OF U.S. AMBASSADOR CAROLINE KENNEDY
A NEW BRIDGE BETWEEN JAPAN AND THE U.S.

ISBN: 978-1-937673-63-5
$14.95 (Paperback)

CONTENTS

FOR THE FUTURE OF THAILAND AND JAPAN

INTERVIEWING THE GUARDIAN SPIRIT OF YINGLUCK SHINAWATRA

ISBN: 978-1-937673-59-8

$14.95 (Paperback)

In December 2013, Thailand's Prime Minister Yingluck announced the dissolution of the nation's parliament and called a snap election to be held in February 2014. But this did not appease the thousands of angry protestors who remained on the streets of Bangkok. During this time of social unrest, Prime Minister Yingluck were mostly absent from Bangkok to avoid protestors, spending more time in the Northern and Northeastern areas. It was in such a difficult time for the prime minister and the country of Thailand that Master Ryuho Okawa conducted a spiritual interview with Prime Minister Yingluck. In this spiritual interview, the guardian spirit of Prime Minister Yingluck shares her views on many controversial topics including democracy in Thailand, Thailand's relationships with China and Japan, traditional Buddhism, and Islam. She then asks Japan to help her country which has plunged into turmoil. It is Master Ryuho Okawa's hope that this interview will become a bridge to build a wonderful relationship between Thailand and Japan.

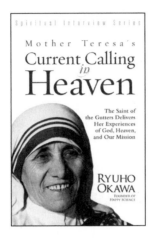

MOTHER TERESA'S CURRENT CALLING IN HEAVEN

THE SAINT OF THE GUTTERS DELIVERS HER EXPERIENCES OF GOD, HEAVEN, AND OUR MISSION

ISBN: 978-1-937673-55-0

$14.95 (Paperback)

This book is a spiritual interview with Mother Teresa's spirit who talks through Master Ryuho Okawa. In this spiritual interview, which was conducted sixteen years after Mother Teresa's death, Mother Teresa's spirit talks about her astonishing discoveries about God, Heaven, and the mission that people on earth should aim to fulfill through life. Mother Teresa reveals that the other world is a vast place with many levels of angels, that Heaven and Hell exist, and that the reality of the human being is the soul. In addition to a discussion about the contradictions within Christian teachings and the need for new teachings for today's people, she also talks about her discoveries about God and Jesus Christ, and says that it is the mission of the wealthy to help others who are in poverty, through prayer and a pure heart.

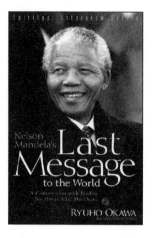

NELSON MANDELA'S LAST MESSAGE

A CONVERSATION WITH MADIBA
SIX HOURS AFTER HIS DEATH

ISBN: 978-1-937673-53-6
$14.95 (Paperback)

On December 5, 2013, the entire world mourned the passing of Nelson Mandela. Even as the news was spreading, Mandela's spirit came to Master Ryuho Okawa to give us all an important message of hope and to prove that the afterlife exists. Archbishop of Canterbury Justin Wilby paid this tribute to the first black president of South Africa and the man who liberated his country from apartheid: "His courage was undefeated, indomitable, extraordinary." Perhaps it was Mandela's indomitable belief in the fundamental reality of the human soul that gave him such extraordinary courage in the face of adversity. For as he says in this spiritual interview, God created our souls as thinking energy without color, and that our colorless soul is the basis of our fundamental freedom and equality. In this spiritual interview, Master Ryuho Okawa gives us a glimpse into the mind of this great leader whose undefeated spirit is a message of hope to us all.

SOUTH KOREA'S CONSPIRACY
PRESIDENT PARK'S HIDDEN AGENDA TO UNITE WITH CHINA

ISBN: 978-1-937673-51-2
$14.95 (Paperback)

On June 27, 2013, South Korea's President Park Geun-hye and Chinese President Xi Jinping held summit talks in Beijing. At the meeting, President Park asked China's Xi Jinping to build a memorial of An Jung-geun, the man who in 1909 assassinated the first Prime Minister of Japan and the first Resident-General of Korea, Ito Hirobumi. In this spiritual interview, we begin by speaking with the spirit of An Jung-geun before moving on to a conversation with the guardian spirit of President Park, who forced herself into the interview out of fear that the interview will reveal the truth about him. Through these conversations, Master Ryuho Okawa tries to discover the facts about the assassination of Ito Hirobumi to determine whether An Jung-geun can justifiably be hailed as a hero. While South Koreans continue to accuse Japan of having wronged their nation, Master Okawa hopes that these interviews will provide a truthful understanding of the historical events between Japan and South Korea and help the international community understand the nature of true international justice.

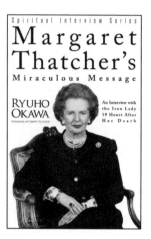

MARGARET THATCHER'S
MIRACULOUS MESSAGE
An Interview with the Iron Lady
19 Hours After Her Death

ISBN: 978-1-937673-37-6
$14.95 (Paperback)

On April 9, 2013, just nineteen hours after Margaret Thatcher's death, Master Ryuho Okawa summoned her spirit to hold a miraculous spiritual interview with Europe's first female prime minister, famously known as the Iron Lady. In words marked by her signature clarity and determination, Margaret Thatcher provided valuable answers to essential and timely questions. Her answers will prove helpful not only to the United Kingdom, but also to the global economy and governments all over the world, including those of the United States and the European Union.

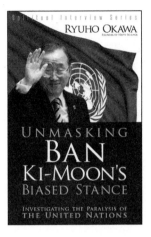

UNMASKING BAN KI-MOON'S
BIASED STANCE
INVESTIGATING THE PARALYSIS OF THE UNITED NATIONS

ISBN: 978-1-937673-49-9
$14.95 (Paperback)

The world is currently facing many critical international issues that require resolution through strong leadership dedicated to the preservation of international peace and security. What are U.N. Secretary-General Ban Ki-moon's true thoughts on these pressing issues? What does he think about the disputes between Japan and South Korea over ownership of the Takeshima Islands, between Japan and China over ownership of the Senkaku Islands, and between Iran and Israel over nuclear weapons capability? Can we depend on him to successfully uphold the principle of impartiality in the United Nations's role of peacemaking? In this spiritual interview with the guardian spirit of Mr. Ban Ki-moon, Master Okawa reveals the U.N. Secretary-General's true character and true intentions regarding his important peacemaking responsibilities.

STEVE JOBS RETURNS
WITH HIS SECRETS
BE SIMPLE, BE CRAZY

ISBN: 978-1-937673-47-5
$19.95 (Paperback)

In this spiritual interview with Steve Jobs, conducted just three months after his death, Master Okawa offers us a chance to catch a glimpse into the mind of one of America's modern geniuses, whom President Barack Obama has described as one among the greatest American innovators. What was the aesthetic philosophy behind his passionate drive to create products that he described as "at the intersection of art and technology?" What were the secrets to his creativity and the successful sales of his products? As Master Okawa often says, and as this interview with the mind of one of the greatest modern innovators will show you, success is always in the way we think and in the substance of our goals and ideals.

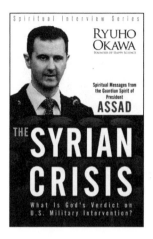

THE SYRIAN CRISIS
WHAT IS GOD'S VERDICT ON U.S. MILITARY INTERVENTION?

ISBN: 978-1-937673-44-4
$14.95 (Paperback)

Is there justice in a U.S. military intervention into the
ongoing Syrian crisis? What is God's perspective on the
tragedy that is occurring in Syria? In *The Syrian Crisis: What
Is God's Verdict on U.S. Military Intervention?* Master Ryuho
Okawa conducts a spiritual interview with the guardian
spirit of Bashar al-Assad. As this interview reveals, the Syrian
dictator's true character is quite different from what we saw
in the CBS interview. As the world braces for a possible
world war, Master Ryuho Okawa provides us with a clear
sense of where God's justice lies in this international crisis.

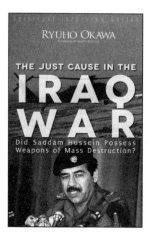

THE JUST CAUSE IN THE IRAQ WAR

DID SADDAM HUSSEIN POSSESS
WEAPONS OF MASS DESTRUCTION?

ISBN: 978-1-937673-41-3
$14.95 (Paperback)

The Just Cause in the Iraq War: Did Saddam Hussein Possess Weapons of Mass Destruction? tackles one of the most controversial and pertinent issues in international politics today. Is President Obama correct that the Iraq War was an unjust war, as he claimed during the 2012 presidential race? Did Saddam Hussein truly have no weapons of mass destruction, or are those weapons still hidden in Iraq, somewhere beyond the reach of U.S. intelligence? In this book, you will discover that Saddam Hussein was also behind the planning of the 9/11 terrorist attacks and both he and Osama bin Laden are now in Hell. The knowledge this book provides will help each of us make the right decisions as we work together to create a peaceful international society.

FORECASTING THE SECOND KOREAN WAR
HOW WILL THE WORLD HANDLE THE CRISIS?

ISBN: 978-1-937673-35-2
$14.95 (Paperback)

Forecasting the Second Korean War: How Will the World Handle the Crisis? forecasts a potential crisis that the United States, South Korea, and Japan may face. In part 1, Master Okawa draws on the help of Edgar Cayce to describe in detail the unfolding of a second Korean War that could begin in the summer of 2013. Part 2 of this book contains a spiritual interview with Kim Il Sung that reveals that he is spiritually guiding Kim Jong Un. Together, the two parts of this book reveal the shocking fact that the crisis on the Korean peninsula is only a small part of a larger and more global imperialistic scheme that is being masterminded by Xi Jinping, the president of China. You will discover who is truly behind the Islamist terrorist attacks against the United States.

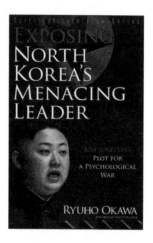

EXPOSING NORTH KOREA'S MENACING LEADER

KIM JONG UN'S PLOT FOR A PSYCHOLOGICAL WAR

ISBN: 978-1-937673-39-0

$14.95 (Paperback)

Exposing North Korea's Menacing Leader: Kim Jong Un's Plot for a Psychological War reveals the role that North Korea is playing in China's imperialistic strategy and the two nations' close ties with Iran. Together, China and Kim Jong Un—North Korea's supreme leader— are carrying out a psychological war that takes full advantage of the weaknesses of Japanese Prime Minister Abe and United States President Obama. Indeed, this interview with Kim Jong Un's guardian spirit reveals that Kim Jong Un was most likely behind the Boston marathon bombings that occurred on April 15, 2013.

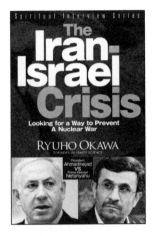

THE IRAN-ISRAEL CRISIS

LOOKING FOR A WAY TO PREVENT A NUCLEAR WAR

ISBN: 978-1-937673-26-0
$14.95 (Paperback)

Master Ryuho Okawa firmly believes that the power to create lasting global peace will come from embracing love and forgiveness beyond differences in religion. This set of spiritual interviews with the guardian spirits of Iran's President Mahmoud Ahmadinejad and Israel's Prime Minister Benjamin Netanyahu reveal their living counterparts' underlying ideas about each other's nations as arch enemies. You will discover hints to solving long-standing clashes between religions.

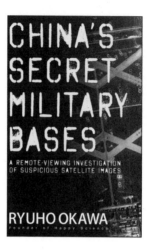

CHINA'S SECRET MILITARY BASES

A REMOTE-VIEWING INVESTIGATION
OF SUSPICIOUS SATELLITE IMAGES

ISBN: 978-1-937673-24-6
$14.95 (Paperback)

Master Okawa reveals China's versions of Area 51 from mysterious satellite photos that had aroused worldwide curiosity. Even American intelligence will be shocked to find out these truths about a hidden enormous missile-launching site full of nuclear warheads prepared to strike major cities around the world. This book is a must-read for anyone who wants to save the world from a full-out nuclear war.

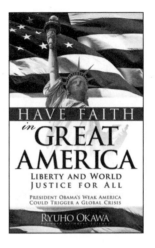

HAVE FAITH IN GREAT AMERICA
LIBERTY AND WORLD JUSTICE FOR ALL

ISBN: 978-1-937673-20-8
$14.95 (Paperback)

Have Faith in Great America: Liberty and World Justice for All is Master Ryuho Okawa's earnest message to the United States of America. The world's future depends on America's fulfillment of its long-held sacred mission of protecting the faith, liberty, and justice of people and nations around the world, and on the development of strong bonds between the United States and Japan.

CHINA'S HIDDEN AGENDA
THE MASTERMIND BEHIND THE ANTI-AMERICAN
AND ANTI-JAPANESE PROTESTS

ISBN: 978-1937673-18-5
$14.95 (Paperback)

"Anti-American demonstrations have been raging in over twenty Arab countries. The man pulling the strings behind all this is Xi Jinping."

—Master Ryuho Okawa

"I wanted to stir up the anti-American movement in the Arab world to make sure that the United States won't be able to attack Syria or Iran…I'm the mastermind behind the Muhammad video."

—Xi Jinping's Guardian Spirit

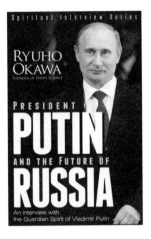

PRESIDENT PUTIN AND
THE FUTURE OF RUSSIA

An Interview with the Guardian Spirit
of Vladimir Putin

ISBN: 978-1-937673-14-7
$14.95 (Paperback)

"I have no intention of fighting the United States. The Cold War is over... I have no intention of fighting the Americans... And I'm not friendly enough with China to think about joining them against the United States... I have given Russians religious freedom, which makes me very different from the Chinese."

—Putin's Guardian Spirit